The Faithful Ghost and Other Tall Tales

LEVEL THREE 1000 HEADWORDS

Great Clarendon Street, Oxford OX2 6DP

Oxford University Press is a department of the University of Oxford. It furthers the University's objective of excellence in research, scholarship, and education by publishing worldwide in

Oxford New York

Auckland Cape Town Dar es Salaam Hong Kong Karachi Kuala Lumpur Madrid Melbourne Mexico City Nairobi New Delhi Shanghai Taipei Toronto

With offices in

Argentina Austria Brazil Chile Czech Republic France Greece Guatemala Hungary Italy Japan Poland Portugal Singapore South Korea Switzerland Thailand Turkey Ukraine Vietnam

First published in Dominoes 2008

2020

16

ISBN: 978 0 19 424825 9 BOOK

ISBN: 978 0 19 463978 1 BOOK AND AUDIO PACK

Printed in China

This book is printed on paper from certified and well-managed sources.

ACKNOWLEDGEMENTS

Illustrations and cover by: Zdenko Basic/The Bright Agency

The publisher would like to thank the following for permission to reproduce photographs: Alamy Stock Photo pp ivb (Edith Nesbit/Mary Evans Picture Library), ivc (Jerome K Jerome/Classic Image), 12 (plate camera/Antiques & Collectables), 73 (Dover Castle/Martin Beddall); Bridgeman Images p60 (Field of Yellow Irises at Giverny, 1887 (oil on canvas), Monet, Claude (1840-1926)/Musee Marmottan Monet, Paris, France); Corbis pp ive (Rudyard Kipling/Corbis), 28 (Wurzburg/Jose Fuste Raga), 37 (1884 Illustration of Strawberry Hill Manor/Historical Picture Archive), 74 (Vanderbilt Family Mausoleum/Bettmann); Getty Images pp iva (Washington Irving/Bob Thomas/Popperfoto), ivd (M.R. James/Hulton Archive); iStockphoto pp7 (tombstone/bns124), 21 (Fortress Marienberg/Exkalibur), 61 (cemetery/onfilm), 61 (graveyard/MTealRodgers), 61 (pumpkins/Lisa Thornberg), 61 (cottage/fotoVoyager), 61 (sale advert/trianide), 61 (Stone Celtic Cross/George Clerk), 61 (pipe/SensorSpot), 72 (lighthouse/percussionist); Mary Evans Picture Library p52 (public transport in Paris/BeBa/Iberfoto); OUP pp61 (lightning/Digital Vision), 61 (cottage/mubus7), 74 (derelict mansion/Antlio); Shutterstock pp37 (ghosts/Albo003), 61 (columns/Elena Kharichkina).

DOMINOES

Series Editors: Bill Bowler and Sue Parminter

The Faithful Ghost and Other Tall Tales

Retold by Bill Bowler

Illustrated by Zdenko Basic

Ghost stories and tall tales have always interested Bill Bowler. This collection contains stories by two of the finest tellers of ghostly tales in English – Washington Irving and M. R. James. Also included are three excellent ghost stories by writers who are perhaps more famous for other types of tale – J. K. Jerome, Rudyard Kipling, and E. Nesbit. You will find exciting, sad, strange, and amusing stories in this book. But if you are easily frightened, be sure to read them in the light of day – not late at night, alone.

OXFORD
UNIVERSITY PRESS

About the Authors

Washington Irving (1783–1859) was born – the youngest of 11 children – in New York, the United States. He studied law, but worked for only a short time. He lived in Europe for many years, and was the first world famous American writer. He is best known as the writer of *Rip Van Winkle* and *The Legend of Sleepy Hollow*, also available as a Dominoes reader.

Edith Nesbit (1858–1924) was born in London, England. She went to school in France and Germany where she was very unhappy. In 1871 she moved back to England and started writing. Edith married and had children, but also wrote. She is best remembered today for her children's stories, of which one of the most famous is *The Railway Children* (1906).

Jerome Klapka Jerome (1859–1927) was born in Staffordshire in central England. His childhood was difficult as his parents were poor and died when he was 13. He took jobs working for the railways, as a journalist, a teacher and an actor. He wrote stories all this time but he only became famous with *Three Men in a Boat* (1889), an amusing story of a boat journey on the river Thames.

Montague Rhodes James (1862–1936) was born in Kent, England. He was a brilliant student at Cambridge University and later taught there. M. R. James also wrote some of the greatest ghost stories in English. He started writing them to amuse friends, and every Christmas Eve read a new story aloud to them. He published five books of ghost stories.

Rudyard Kipling (1865–1936) was born in Bombay (now Mumbai) in India to English parents. He loved listening to Indian rhymes and stories as a child. When he was six he went to school in England. In 1881 he returned to live in India and started work as a journalist. He travelled widely as a journalist and a fiction writer, and lived in both the USA and England. His most famous book is *The Jungle Book* (1894).

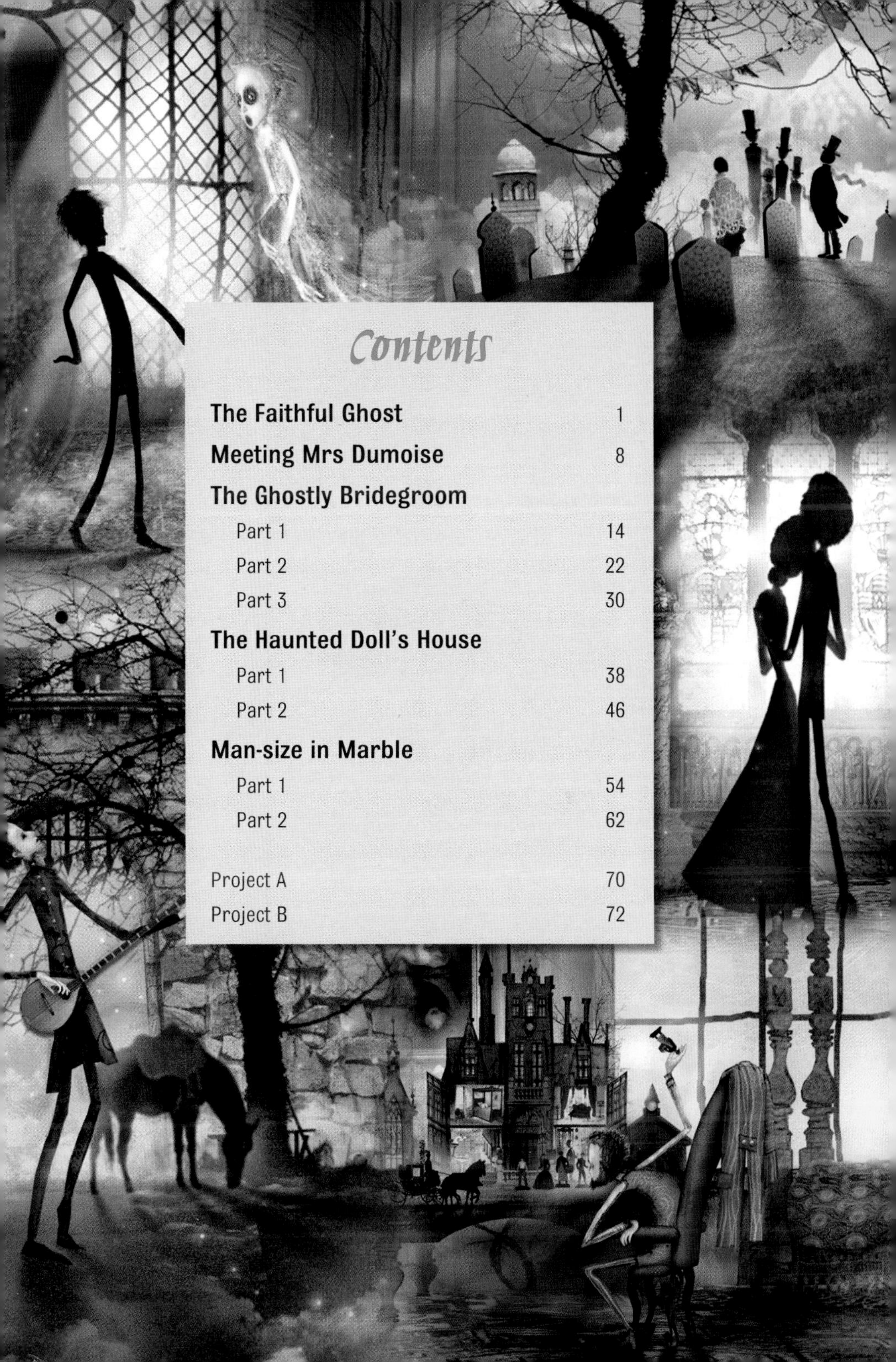

Contents

ACTIVITIES

BEFORE READING

1 You often find these things in ghost stories. Match the words with the pictures Use a dictionary to help you.

a a grave
b a candle
c a churchyard
d a coffin
e a tomb
f poison
g a chapel
h a cross

2 Match the titles of the stories on the Contents page with these summaries.

a Some dolls show the owner of an old doll's house a terrible story.
b The ghost of a man's dead wife comes to warn him about something.
c A young couple move to a country village. As Halloween gets near, they hear a terrible story about two knights whose marble tombs are in the church nearby.
d A handsome young man is on his way to get married when he is killed. Later people see his ghost meet his future bride.
e An old ghost haunts the house where his love once lived. The people who live there plan to make him leave.

3 Do you know any ghost stories? Tell a partner.

The Faithful Ghost

by J. K. Jerome

I was little more than a boy when I first met Johnson. I was home from school for the Christmas holidays and, because it was the night before Christmas my parents let me stay up very late. When I went to my room that night and opened the door, I found myself face to face with Johnson, who was coming out. He passed through me and, giving a long low **moan** of great sadness, he disappeared out of the window by the stairs.

moan a low sad sound that someone makes; to make a low sad sound

For a moment I was very surprised. I was only a schoolboy at the time, I'd never seen a ghost before, and so I felt a little afraid about going to bed. But, thinking about it, I remembered ghosts could hurt only bad people, so I got under the bed covers and went to sleep.

In the morning, I told my father about what I'd seen.

'Oh, yes, that was old Johnson,' he answered. 'Don't be frightened of him; he lives here.' And then he told me the poor thing's life story.

It seemed that Johnson, when he was alive and young, had loved the daughter of a man who'd once owned our house. She was a beautiful young woman and her first name was Emily. Father didn't know her other name.

Johnson was too poor to marry her, so he kissed her goodbye, and said, 'I'll soon be back.' Then he left for Australia to make his **fortune**. But Australia wasn't then what it became later. In those days there weren't many people who travelled across the wide open country there that you could rob and kill. Because of this, it took Johnson nearly twenty years to get all the money he wanted.

But at last the job he'd given himself was done. Escaping from the police and leaving Australia, he returned with his fortune to England – full of great happiness and hope – to ask Emily to marry him.

When he reached the house, he found it silent and empty. None of the neighbours could tell him much. They said that, soon after he himself had left England, the family had disappeared quietly one cold, wet night, and that nobody had ever seen or heard anything of them since then although the **landlord** and many of the owners of nearby shops had tried very hard to find them.

Poor Johnson, crazy with **grief**, had gone to look for his lost love all over the world. He never found her, and after years of unsuccessful searching, he returned to end his lonely life in the same house where, in happy earlier days, he and his dearest Emily had spent so many wonderful hours together.

He'd lived there all alone, walking about crying and calling to his Emily to come back to him. And when the poor old thing had died, his ghost had gone on with the same business.

fortune money, houses and valuable things that make you a rich person

landlord a man who gets money from renting out a house

grief great sadness that you feel after someone that you love dies

'And so,' Father said, 'when I moved into this house, the landlord took ten pounds off the **rent** for me.'

After that, I often met Johnson around the place at all hours of the night, and so did everybody. At first we used to walk round him or stand to one side to let him pass. But when we became more comfortable with him, it didn't seem necessary to be so polite, and we used to walk straight through him. You couldn't say he was ever very much in our way.

He was a gentle old ghost who wouldn't hurt a fly, and we all felt very sorry for him. For a while, indeed, he was a real favourite with the women of the house. He was so **faithful** to his dear Emily, and their hearts were touched by it.

But as time went on, he started to become a little boring. You see, he was full of sadness. There was nothing amusing or pleasant about him. You felt sorry for him, but he **annoyed** you. He used to sit on the stairs and cry for hours at a time. And when we woke up in the middle of the night, we were sure to hear him moving up and down the stairs and in and out of the different rooms, moaning and **sighing**. It really wasn't easy to go back to sleep again. And when we had a party, he used to come and sit outside the **drawing room** door and cry bitterly all the time. He didn't really do anything to hurt anybody, but he made everything a little **depressing**.

'I'm getting tired of that stupid old ghost,' said my father one evening after Johnson had been even more annoying than usual. He was sitting up the chimney, moaning, and had made it impossible for us to think straight while we were playing a game of cards. 'We'll have to get rid of him, one way or another. I wish I knew how to do it.'

'Well,' said my mother. 'You can be sure we'll never see the back of him until he's found Emily's **grave**. That's what he's looking for. Find Emily's grave and let him know where it is, and he'll go and haunt that. It's the only thing to do.'

rent the money that you give every month for a place to live; to give money every month for a place to live

faithful true to your husband or wife and not having other lovers; true to your friends or people that you work for and not forgetting them

annoy to make you feel a little angry

sigh to blow air from your mouth with a sad or tired sound; air that you blow from your mouth with a sad or tired sound

drawing room a living room in a large house

depressing making you feel very unhappy

grave a hole in the ground where you put a dead body

haunt to spend lots of time in a place (often used of ghosts)

The idea seemed reasonable, but the difficulty was that none of us knew where Emily's grave was. Father said that we should find some other Emily's grave and pretend it was the real thing, but, unluckily for us, no Emily of any kind was **buried** anywhere for miles around. I've never seen a place so terribly empty of dead Emilies.

I thought for a while, and then I said, 'Couldn't we just make a grave for Emily in our garden? He doesn't seem to be the cleverest of ghosts. He might **believe** it's the real thing. At least we can try.'

bury to put a dead person under the ground

believe to think that something is true

'All right, let's try it!' said my father. So the next morning we had some workmen in to dig a little grave between the apple trees at the bottom of the garden, and to put a nice white gravestone at one end of it, with these words on it: In loving **memory** of Emily. Her last words were: 'Tell Johnson I love him.'

'That's sure to work,' said Father to himself, and it did.

We made sure that Johnson went down there that same night, and – well – the way he ran and threw his arms round that gravestone, moaning and sighing, was one of the saddest things I've ever seen. Dad and old Squibbins the gardener cried like children when they saw it.

memory what you remember

We've had no more trouble from Johnson in the house since then. He spends every night now crying bitterly on the grave, and seems really pleased.

Is he still there? Oh, yes. I'll take you down and show him to you the next time you come to our place – ten in the evening to four in the morning are his usual hours, ten o'clock to two o'clock on Saturdays.

ACTIVITIES

READING CHECK

1 What do you know about Johnson? Tick the correct column.

	True	False	Don't know
a He was a frightening ghost.	☐	☑	☐
b He loved Christmas.	☐	☐	☐
c His girlfriend had lived in the storyteller's house.	☐	☐	☐
d He went to Australia to find a good job.	☐	☐	☐
e He arrived back in England a rich man.	☐	☐	☐
f When he returned to England Emily was already married.	☐	☐	☐
g He died in the storyteller's house.	☐	☐	☐
h He wanted to frighten the people in the house.	☐	☐	☐
i At first everyone in the house felt sorry for him.	☐	☐	☐
j He cried and made a lot of noise.	☐	☐	☐
k His girlfriend's grave was at the bottom of the garden.	☐	☐	☐
l At the end of the story he stops haunting the house.	☐	☐	☐

WORD WORK

1 Tick the correct word in each sentence.

a The old ghost . . . the house where his girlfriend once lived.
1 ☑ haunts **2** ☐ annoys **3** ☐ buries

b They say that the King . . . his gold under the castle before he died.
1 ☐ moaned **2** ☐ haunted **3** ☐ buried

c Johnson wakes the family with his loud . . . .
1 ☐ grief **2** ☐ moans **3** ☐ sighs

d 'Please don't go,' he . . . , 'I love you.'
1 ☐ sighed **2** ☐ annoyed **3** ☐ buried

e Johnson . . . the family because he is always sad.
1 ☐ haunts **2** ☐ buries **3** ☐ annoys

f Some people say that the old man went crazy with . . . after his wife died.
1 ☐ grave **2** ☐ grief **3** ☐ moans

g No one can find Emily's . . . .
1 ☐ grief **2** ☐ grave **3** ☐ bury

2 Use the words in the gravestone to complete the gaps in Johnson's letter.

My darling Emily,

I came back to England with a (a) fortune in my pockets hoping we could be married. But where were you then, and where are you now? Have you been (b) .... to me, or are you married to someone else?

These days your old (c) .... is letting me live in the house. I pay him (d) ...., of course. I'm writing to you now from the (e) .... where we spent many happy hours together. But it's (f) .... living here alone with only (g) .... of you in my head. I try to (h) .... that one day I will see you once again.

Yours lovingly,
Joe Johnson

believe
depressing
drawing room
faithful
~~fortune~~
landlord
memories
rent

GUESS WHAT

Match the main characters in the next story, *Meeting Mrs Dumoise* with the phrases below.

- **a** ☐ dies soon after the story begins.
- **b** ☐ sees a ghost.
- **c** ☐ is a doctor.
- **d** ☐ is very frightened.
- **e** ☐ is very sad when his wife dies.
- **f** ☐ gives Ram Dass a message.

1 ***Dumoise***

2 ***Mrs Dumoise***

3 ***Ram Dass***

Meeting Mrs Dumoise

by Rudyard Kipling

This story can be explained by people who know about ghosts. I've lived long enough in India to know it's best just to tell things the way they happened.

Dumoise worked as our doctor at Meridki in the Punjab, in the north-west of India. He was a round, sleepy little man, and he married a young woman as round and sleepy-looking as himself. After their wedding they forgot about the rest of the world and were very happy. Life in Meridki went on quite well without them.

But Dumoise was wrong to shut himself away from the world, as he discovered when there was an **epidemic** of **typhoid** in Meridki, and his wife became ill with the **disease**. Five days were lost before he realized she had more than just a **fever**. Three more days passed before he visited Mrs Shute, the engineer's wife, and spoke to her in a **nervous** way about his trouble. She almost hit him round the ears.

'It's a crime you waited so long to tell someone,' she said, and went off immediately to care for the poor woman. Seven people in Meridki caught typhoid that winter, and for fifty-six days we fought the disease and brought them back to the world of the living.

Just when we thought it was all finished, little Mrs Dumoise became worse again, and died in less than a week. Everyone went to the **funeral**. Dumoise started crying at the edge of the grave and was taken away by friends at once.

After his wife's death, Dumoise went back to their house alone. He didn't want help. He did his job well, but we all told him he should take a holiday. Dumoise was grateful for the idea, and went to the hills in north-east India, on a walking tour.

He took a gun and a big camera with him, hoping to take lots of photographs and forget his grief. A useless Indian **servant**

Dumoise /du'mwa:z/

epidemic when a lot of people have the same illness at the same time

typhoid an illness where you get a bad stomach, a fever, and red spots on your body

disease illness

fever when you get very hot because you are ill

nervous a little afraid

funeral the time when a dead person is put under the ground

servant a person who works for someone rich

went with him, to help with his luggage. The man was lazy and not very honest, but he'd been his wife's favourite and most faithful servant, and Dumoise was happy to let him manage everything.

On his way back from the hills, Dumoise went to a place called Bagi. The house where walkers can stay there is open to the winds and a bitterly cold place. He stopped at seven o'clock in the evening, and his servant went down the hillside into the village to find carriers for the next day. The sun had gone down, and it was windy. Dumoise stood in front of the house, waiting for the man to come back. He returned almost immediately, and so quickly that Dumoise thought he'd probably met some wild animal on the way. He was running as hard as he could up the side of the hill.

When he reached Dumoise, he fell down at his feet. Blood came from his nose and his face was grey with fear. Then he said, 'I've seen the **Memsahib**.'

Memsahib the word Indian servants used for a British woman

'Where?' asked Dumoise.

'Down on the road to the village. She was in a blue dress, and she looked at me from under her hat and said, "Ram Dass, say hello to my husband and tell him I'll meet him next month at Nuddea." Then I ran away because I felt very afraid.'

I don't know what Dumoise did. Ram Dass said he walked up and down in front of the house and waited for the Memsahib to come up the hill, holding out his arms in front of him like someone who was crazy. But no Memsahib came, and the next day Dumoise travelled onwards to Simla, the summer home of the British **government** in northern India. He asked Ram Dass endless questions about what had happened to him in Bagi along the way.

Ram Dass could only say he'd met Mrs Dumoise, she'd looked at him from under her hat, and had said the words he'd reported. He never changed his story.

'I don't know where Nuddea is, I've never been to Nuddea, and I don't want to go there, even if I'm paid twice what I usually get to go,' he added.

Nuddea is in Bengal in southern India. It has nothing to do with a doctor working in the Punjab. It's more than twelve hundred miles south of Meridki, where Dumoise lived.

Dumoise passed through Simla without stopping, and then went on to Meridki. There he met the doctor who'd taken his

government
the people who control a country

place at the hospital while he was away. This man was an old friend of his, and they talked for a day about work. In the evening Dumoise told the man what had happened at Bagi.

At that moment the **telegram** boy ran in with a telegram from the government offices in Simla. Dumoise read it with interest. It said:

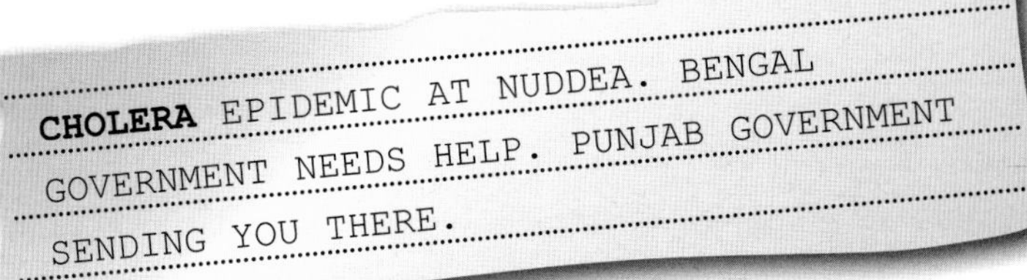
CHOLERA EPIDEMIC AT NUDDEA. BENGAL GOVERNMENT NEEDS HELP. PUNJAB GOVERNMENT SENDING YOU THERE.

Dumoise threw the telegram on the table. 'Well!' he cried.

The other doctor said nothing. What could he say?

Then he remembered Dumoise had passed through Simla.

'Did you hear about this already and take the job in order to make an end of your–?' he began, but Dumoise stopped him.

'Not at all. It's the first I've heard of it. But if death comes for me, I won't be sorry.'

In the half-light the other man helped to put Dumoise's things back in his bags. Ram Dass came in with a light.

'Where's the **Sahib** going?' he asked.

'To Nuddea,' answered Dumoise softly.

At that, Ram Dass fell to the floor, pulling at Dumoise's legs and asking him not to go. He cried and moaned until he was told to leave the room. Then he put all his things together and came to ask for a **reference**.

'I'm not going to Nuddea to see the Sahib die, and perhaps die myself,' he said.

So Dumoise paid him, gave him a reference, and went to Nuddea alone. Eleven days later he'd joined his Memsahib, and the Bengal government had to find a new doctor to fight the epidemic in Nuddea. For Dumoise lay dead from cholera in the hospital there.

telegram a very short letter that you send very quickly

cholera a stomach illness you get from drinking dirty water, which can kill you

Sahib the word Indian servants used for a British man

reference a letter from a past employer saying how well you work that you can show when you are looking for a job

ACTIVITIES

READING CHECK

Read the summary of *Meeting Mrs Dumoise* and cross out nine more extra pieces of information not in the story.

Dumoise was a doctor ~~in a modern hospital~~ in the north of India. He married Mrs Dumoise one beautiful summer day and they were both very happy. Although Dumoise was a very good doctor, his wife got ill and died from a bad disease. After her death Dumoise went on holiday for a month in the Indian hills to forget his grief. He took his camera, his gun and his wife's favourite servant with him, a lazy man with six children called Ram Dass. One windy evening, on their way home from the hills, Ram Dass saw Mrs Dumoise's ghost. She was wearing a blue dress and she looked very sad. She gave him a message for her husband; to meet her on the first Monday of the next month in a place called Nuddea. Nuddea was a large town in the south of India, a long way from Dumoise's home. When they returned home, Dumoise told another doctor about his wife's ghost . While they were speaking in the garden, he got a message from the government about a new job in the south of India. It was in Nuddea. Mr Dumoise travelled to Nuddea with some other servants, but without Ram Dass. Eleven days later, he died there of a bad disease.

WORD WORK

Rewrite each sentence with a word from the camera instead of the underlined words.

a Are you <u>a little afraid</u> about the exam tomorrow?

Are you nervous about the exam tomorrow?

b He died last week and his <u>time to be buried</u> is today.

c More than 200 <u>men and women</u> work in the palace.

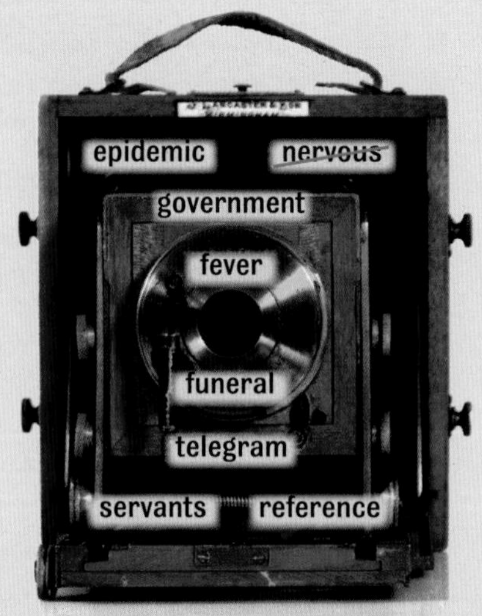

d I've got a hot head and feel ill today. Yuk!

e Excuse me, I want to send a short, quick message to Australia.

f I have to write an essay about Myanmar life and the people who control the country.

g We're not going to Vietnam because of the flu that a lot of people have there.

h Please send a letter about you from your boss if you are interested in the job.

GUESS WHAT

The next story is called *The Ghostly Bridegroom*. Which two sentences do you think are true about each of the main characters at the beginning of the story?

a The bride . . .

- **1** ☐ lives in a castle in a forest.
- **2** ☐ is waiting to meet her future husband.
- **3** ☐ really doesn't want to get married.

b The bridegroom . . .

- **1** ☐ really doesn't want to get married.
- **2** ☐ is killed by some thieves.
- **3** ☐ is excited about meeting his future bride.

c The bride's father . . .

- **1** ☐ arranges his daughter's marriage.
- **2** ☐ isn't a kind man.
- **3** ☐ loves telling ghost stories.

d The bridegroom's friend . . .

- **1** ☐ hates adventures.
- **2** ☐ is the son of one of the bride's father's enemies.
- **3** ☐ makes a promise to his dying friend.

The Ghostly Bridegroom – Part 1

by Washington Irving

A long time ago, on a mountain in the Odenwald – that forested part of southern Germany where the Main river meets the Rhine – **Baron** Von Landshort's castle stood. These days nearly nothing is left of it, but in those days it looked down on the country around it – like its owner.

The baron was a **proud** man from the Katzenellenbogen family. His father, a great army man, had left him the castle, and the baron took care of it as well as he could.

Other old German families had sold their uncomfortable castles in the hills and built more comfortable houses in the valleys. But the baron stayed and continued with the old family ways. This meant he often argued with his neighbours, because his **ancestors** had once disagreed with theirs.

The baron had only one child, a beautiful daughter. Two unmarried aunts cared for her when she was a child, and taught her all the important things a young lady should know.

baron an important man from a good German family

proud feeling that you are more important than other people; happy about something that you have done or can do

ancestor a person from your family in the past

By the time she was eighteen, she could read without trouble. She could also write her name without forgetting a single letter – and big enough for her aunts to read without their glasses. She could dance, play the guitar, and sing several beautiful love songs from memory, too.

Her aunts, who had lived for love when they were young, always kept a careful eye on her, and made sure she never got into trouble. She never left the castle alone, and had to listen to endless talks about the importance of politeness.

'You must always obey your father,' one aunt told her.

'Never get close to men, and never believe a word they say,' said the other.

Her aunts felt sure that, although other young women might make mistakes in matters of love, this would never happen to the baron's daughter.

'Without her father's **approval**, she won't look twice at the best-looking young man in the world, even if he's dying at her feet,' they thought.

Plenty of other people lived in the baron's castle with him. He had many poorer **relatives** who often visited him for big family parties paid for by the baron.

They always told him after a few drinks, 'There's nothing more enjoyable than our visits to your home.'

The baron was a small man with a big heart. He loved telling stories about the brave old Katzenellenbogen fighters who stared down proudly from their pictures on the castle walls. His special favourites were ghost stories. Each story he told was always listened to happily by his poor relatives, even if it was the hundredth time they'd heard it.

This was the baron's life. He was like a king in his castle, and believed himself to be the cleverest man in the world.

approval thinking that something is good

relative a person in your family

On the day when my story begins, the baron had planned a big party in the castle to **celebrate** the arrival of his daughter's future **bridegroom**.

The baron and a very grand old man from one of the finest families in Bavaria had decided to join their fortunes together by marrying their children to each other. Letters of great politeness were sent and replied to. Although they hadn't even seen each other, the young pair were **engaged** to be married, and the date for the wedding was decided.

Young **Count** von Altenburg had left the army in order to come and fetch his **bride** from the baron's castle. Earlier he'd sent a letter from the nearest city, which the baron had read with interest:

Friday, Wurtzburg

Sir,

I have some business to finish here in Wurtzburg which has made me later than I planned, but I'll arrive soon.

Von Altenburg

Now everyone in the castle was making things ready for the young man's arrival. The future bride was wearing her finest clothes. Her two aunts had argued all morning about every single thing she should wear, so she'd left them arguing and had chosen her clothes herself. Luckily she had good taste. She looked as lovely as any young bridegroom could wish for, and her excitement meant that her pink face and shining eyes made her look even more beautiful than usual.

Her sighs and the dreamy look in her eyes all told of the gentle hopes and fears that fought together in her little heart. And now her aunts were at her side, telling her what to do and what to say to her lover when he arrived. Unmarried aunts are always good at that kind of thing!

celebrate to do something special on an important day

bridegroom a man on the day that he marries

engaged when two people agree that they are going to marry

count a man who is more important than a baron

bride a woman on the day that she marries

The baron was running worriedly here and there, telling his servants to take care with this or that. He had nothing special to do, but was a naturally active man who hated sitting still when all around him were in a hurry.

The castle kitchen was full of food, and a small cow was cooking on the fire, together with the fattest birds from the nearby forest. The most excellent drinks the baron had to offer were all ready for the young count to taste.

But the young bridegroom was late. After some hours, the sun began to disappear behind the mountain tops. The baron climbed to the highest room in the castle and looked out of the window, hoping to see the count and his servants coming along the mountain road.

Once he thought he *could* see them, but it was only some men on horses who went past his castle. In the end, it became too dark for the baron to see the road clearly.

While all this was happening, in a different part of the Odenwald forest, two young men were riding along. One was Count Von Altenburg, who was going unhurriedly to meet his future bride. The other was a good army friend of his – Herman von Starkenfaust – whom he'd met by chance in Wurtzburg.

Starkenfaust was one of the strongest, bravest men in Germany. He was returning from the army to his father's castle. This was close to Baron Landshort's home, although their two families never spoke because their ancestors had argued long ago.

The two young men were travelling the same way, so they agreed to ride onwards together.

The count told his servants, 'You can follow and catch up with me later.'

Then he rode off with his friend through the forest. On the way they first talked happily about their memories of army life. Then the count became a little boring when he started speaking about his future bride.

'Everyone says she's so beautiful, and I'm really looking forward to married life,' he said.

In those days German forests were as full of robbers as German castles were full of ghosts. So it's not surprising that, when they reached the loneliest part of the Odenwald, they were **attacked** by a group of thieves. Both fought bravely, but soon they were losing the battle.

Just then, the count's servants arrived and ran to help them. The criminals ran away. But before leaving, one of them pushed his knife deep into the count's side, leaving him badly hurt on the forest floor.

Slowly and carefully his servants carried him back to the city of Wurtzburg. There they took him to a man of the church who was also famous for his doctorly **skill**, but it was too late for half of the man's skills to be of any use. No medicines could save the young count now. He was dying.

His last words were to the friend who stood at his bedside.

'Go at once to the castle of Landshort and explain why I couldn't come to meet my bride.'

He wasn't perhaps the most loving of lovers, but he was a serious young man, and asked Starkenfaust to give the sad news as nicely as possible.

'If you don't, I won't rest in my grave.' he said.

'I'll do what you ask,' Starkenfaust promised, giving the dying man his hand.

The count took it and held it for a while, but soon he became feverish, and began talking crazily.

'I mustn't break my promise. I must ride to Landshort myself to meet my bride.'

He died while he was trying to get out of bed, run out of the door and jump onto his horse.

Starkenfaust cried a little over his friend's early death. Then he began to think of the difficult job he'd agreed to do.

'How can I visit the castle of my father's enemy unasked,

attack to start hitting someone suddenly

skill knowing how to do something well

bringing depressing news that will destroy his hopes and happiness?' he said to himself.

cathedral a big important church

On the other hand, he was very interested in meeting this young Katzenellenbogen woman whom people said was so beautiful, and who was kept locked away from the world in her father's castle. He loved beautiful women, and he enjoyed adventures.

Before leaving Wurtzburg, he arranged for the count's funeral to take place in the **cathedral**, where several of Von Altenburg's relatives were buried. The rest he left to the young man's servants.

ACTIVITIES

READING CHECK

Put these events from Part 1 of *The Ghostly Bridegroom* in order.

a ☐ Altenburg meets an old friend, Herman von Starkenfaust, in Wurtzburg.
b [1] The baron arranges his daughter's marriage to Count von Altenburg.
c ☐ Altenburg rides through the Odenwald forest with Starkenfaust.
d ☐ Altenburg sends a message to the baron saying he will arrive late.
e ☐ Altenburg asks Starkenfaust to say sorry to the baron's daughter from him.
f ☐ Altenburg's servants take him back to Wurtzburg; Starkenfaust follows.
g ☐ A group of thieves attacks Altenburg and Starkenfaust.
h ☐ A thief pushes a knife into Altenburg's side.
i ☐ Altenburg's servants arrive in the forest.
j ☐ Starkenfaust organizes Altenburg's funeral.
k ☐ Altenburg tries to jump out of bed onto his horse and dies.

WORD WORK

1 Correct the sentences about the pictures with words from *The Ghostly Bridegroom*.

a The washroom and pride are having their photos taken. bridegroom ... bride.
b We had a big party with all our revolutions. ....
c There are paintings of all the king's anchors on the walls. ....
d The carnival opens at nine o'clock. ....

2 Make words to complete the sentences using the word bit square.

~~pr~~	en	ta	val
ill	ap	gag	rate
pro	cel	~~oud~~	ck
ed	at	eb	sk

a The baron was a proud man.

b Are you going to __________ your birthday with a party?

c The thieves were waiting in the forest to ______ the count and his friend.

d You need _____ to play some card games well.

e My boyfriend and I are ________, and we're getting married next year.

f Many young people in India can't marry without their parents' _________.

GUESS WHAT

Which two things happen in the next part of the story?

a ☐ A ghostly figure visits Baron Landshort's castle.

b ☐ The count's funeral takes place in Wurtzburg Cathedral.

c ☐ The baron's daughter runs into the forest and meets a ghost.

d ☐ Starkenfaust breaks his promise and goes straight home to his father.

The Ghostly Bridegroom – Part 2

Now let's return to the Katzenellenbogen family, who were waiting for their **guest** – and for their dinner. Night came, and still the count hadn't arrived. Their dinner couldn't wait. The meats were nearly burnt, the cook was half worried to death, and everyone in the castle had hungry faces, like soldiers who hadn't eaten for months.

In the end, the baron gave orders for the meal to begin immediately. Everyone was just sitting down at the table, when suddenly they heard the sound of a **horn** at the castle **gate**. A stranger was outside, asking to enter. Quickly the baron went to welcome his future **son-in-law**.

The gate opened, and the stranger, horn in hand, waited outside. He was a tall, fine-looking young man on a black horse. His face was pale, but he had shining mysterious eyes and a look of proud sadness about him.

The baron was surprised to see he'd come alone, without any servants. At first he felt annoyed.

'Doesn't that young man realize this is an important visit, and an important family he's marrying into?'

But then he calmed down, saying to himself, 'His youthful excitement has made him hurry here before his servants.'

'I'm sorry,' began the stranger, getting down from his horse, 'to arrive like this at this hour–'

The baron stopped him from saying more by welcoming him warmly and politely. He was proud of his own skill at speaking. Once or twice the stranger tried to stop the river of fine words, but he couldn't. In the end he just looked down at the ground and let it all wash over him.

By the time the baron had finished, they were deep inside the castle. Once more the stranger tried to speak, but this time he was stopped by the arrival of the women of the family, bringing his nervous young bride to meet him. He stared at her for a

guest somebody that you invite to your home, or to a party

horn you blow on this metal instrument to make a long low noise

gate the big door into a castle

son-in-law the man who is married to your daughter

moment like a man in a dream. His eyes shone lovingly as he took in her beautiful face and figure.

One of the unmarried aunts whispered something in the young woman's ear. She tried to speak, lifting her bright blue eyes from the ground to look at her bridegroom nervously, but the words died on her soft lips.

Then she looked back at the floor, although there was now the ghost of a smile on her pretty face, showing she liked what she'd seen. Indeed it was impossible for a young girl of eighteen, who often dreamt of love, not to be pleased by this good-looking young man.

Because their guest had arrived so late, the baron said, 'Let's leave all talk of the wedding until tomorrow.'

He at once invited the young man to join them at the long table in the great hall where dinner waited for them.

From the walls the pictures of the baron's hard-faced ancestors looked down on them as they ate. Next to them there were old battle flags with lots of holes in them, several badly beaten bits of **armour**, and the heads of a number of wild animals from the nearby forest that different Katzenellenbogens had **hunted**, caught, and killed over the centuries.

armour a metal suit that soldiers wore in the past to stop people killing them

hunt to look for animals and birds in order to kill them

The young man didn't take much notice of the other dinner guests, and touched little of the fine meal. He seemed too busy with his bride to think of things like that.

He spoke softly to her in words that those sitting next to them found hard to catch. But a woman can always hear the soft, sweet voice of her lover. His seriousness and gentleness seemed to touch the young lady deeply, and she listened closely to all he said, sometimes smiling and sometimes serious.

From time to time she said something back to him. And when he wasn't looking at her, she watched him out of the corner of her eye and sighed happily.

The two unmarried aunts, who both knew the mysteries of the heart well, told their neighbours at the table, 'We're sure the two of them fell in love the moment they met.'

The dinner went on happily. The baron's poorer relatives ate hungrily, in the way that people with little money do after they've spent days walking in the mountains.

The baron told his best stories with great success. When it was a mystery story, his listeners were suitably surprised, and when it was amusing, they laughed in all the right places.

Other, cleverer relatives told even funnier stories, or whispered things in the ladies' ears that made it hard for them not to laugh. One very happy, round-faced man sang some not very polite songs that made the unmarried aunts' faces turn red.

But instead of enjoying the fun of the party, the bridegroom looked a little out of place. His face became more miserable as the evening went on, and – strangely – the baron's funny stories made him look even sadder.

Sometimes he seemed to forget all around him. At other times he looked round the hall with restless eyes that spoke of an uneasy heart.

His conversations with his bride became more serious and mysterious. Her pretty face became clouded with worry, and she began to shake nervously at his words.

The people sitting near them noticed. They couldn't understand why the bridegroom looked so miserable, but his coldness darkened the warm happiness of all around him.

People began whispering to each other and shaking their heads. Songs and laughs died on people's lips, and there were uncomfortable silences in conversations.

Then people began telling stories about ghosts and other wild figures of the night. Each story was more frightening than the one before it. In the end, the baron made several ladies scream at the now very famous story of the '**goblin** horseman'. He told of how the strange mannish thing on a black horse came quietly one dark midnight and took the beautiful Leonora, the only child of her mother and father, from her room, and how she was never seen again alive after that night.

goblin a strange, man-like being that lives under trees or in rocks and makes problems for people

The bridegroom listened to this story with interest. Just before the baron finished, the young man began to stand up. He grew taller and taller until – to the baron at his side – he seemed like a great mountain of a man standing over him. Immediately the story was finished, the young man sighed deeply and said goodbye to everyone. They were all surprised, and no one was more surprised than the baron himself.

'Are you planning to leave at midnight? But everything's ready for you to stay with us tonight! Please go to your room now if you'd like to lie down.'

The stranger shook his head sadly, saying, 'I must lie in a different place tonight.'

There was something about this answer, and the way it was said, that made the baron's heart stop for a second. But he pulled himself together and again warmly invited the young man to stay.

The stranger shook his head silently. Waving goodbye to everyone, he walked slowly from the hall. The unmarried aunts sat as still as stones, and the bride began to cry.

The baron followed the stranger outside to where his black horse was waiting. As they stood at the castle entrance, the stranger turned and spoke to the baron in a deep, loud voice which the high roof above them made deeper and louder.

'Now we're alone I'll tell you why I must go. I have business that cannot wait which calls me away.'

'Can't you send someone in your place?

'No. I must go myself. I have to be in Wurtzburg Cathedral–'

'Yes, but not now. Tomorrow you'll take your bride and marry her there.'

'No!' replied the stranger, ten times more seriously than before. 'I'm not going to marry. Death is waiting. I'm a dead man. I was killed by robbers. My body lies in Wurtzburg. At midnight they'll bury me. My grave is waiting. I mustn't be late!'

With that, he jumped on his horse, rode across the wooden bridge that took him to the road, and soon disappeared into the dark, windy night.

The baron returned worriedly to the great hall and told everyone there what had happened. Two ladies **fainted**, and others felt sick at the idea that they'd eaten dinner at the same table as a ghost.

Some said, 'Perhaps he's the Wild Hunter.'

faint to fall down suddenly because you are weak, ill, or afraid

He's a famous ghostly figure in many old German stories: a tall, strong, larger-than-life fighter, riding a black horse through the air at midnight. He often calls loudly to the group of noisy big black dogs around him. Their eyes always shine with red fire when they smell the warm meat of lonely travellers still out on the road after dark. The Wild Hunter hunts the living, and a crazy crowd of thin grey figures always dances after him. These are the ghosts of the newly dead – headless, armless, or legless – who moan and bleed helplessly as they're pulled by the Hunter and his dogs through the endless night sky.

Others disagreed with that idea. 'Perhaps he came out of the dark rocky heart of a mountain, or from deep under the ground below an old tree in the forest,' they said.

Anyone who didn't really believe the bridegroom was a terrible ghost or goblin of some kind had to change their ideas the following day. Next morning a letter arrived at the castle explaining about the young count's murder, and his funeral in Wurtzburg Cathedral.

ACTIVITIES

READING CHECK

Match the sentence parts to tell the story of *The Ghostly Bridegroom* – Part 2.

a The bride's family are sitting down to eat
b The first time the bride meets the stranger
c At the dining table the young couple
d As it gets later, the stranger
e After the baron's ghost story, the stranger
f The stranger tells the baron he is going
g The next morning a letter about

1 looks sadder and sadder.
2 the count's death arrives.
3 neither of them talk.
4 when the stranger arrives.
5 to his funeral in Wurtzburg.
6 stands up and leaves.
7 talk together quietly.

WORD WORK

Read the definitions and use the words from the story to complete the crossword.

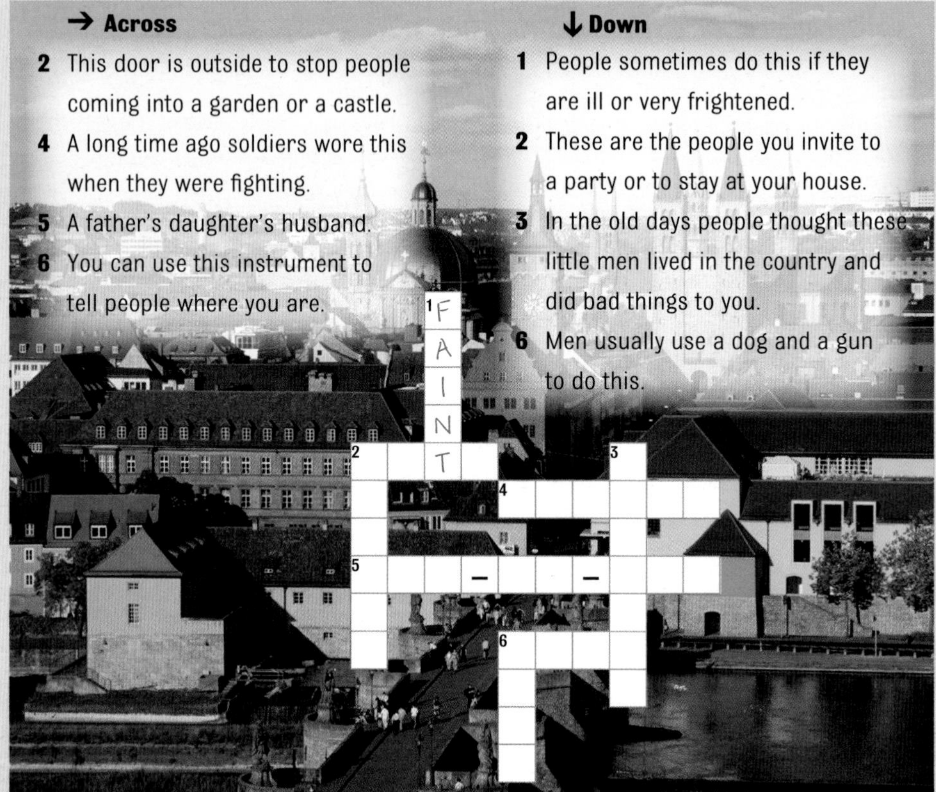

→ Across

2 This door is outside to stop people coming into a garden or a castle.
4 A long time ago soldiers wore this when they were fighting.
5 A father's daughter's husband.
6 You can use this instrument to tell people where you are.

↓ Down

1 People sometimes do this if they are ill or very frightened.
2 These are the people you invite to a party or to stay at your house.
3 In the old days people thought these little men lived in the country and did bad things to you.
6 Men usually use a dog and a gun to do this.

GUESS WHAT

The next chapter is the last part of *The Ghostly Bridegroom*. What do you think happens? Tick the pictures.

a Where does the baron go when he hears of the count's death?

1 ☐ to Wurtzburg cathedral **2** ☐ to the Odenwald forest **3** ☐ to his room

b Who does the bride see in the garden?

1 ☐ Count von Altenburg **2** ☐ the ghostly stranger **3** ☐ a thief

c Who disappears from the castle one week later?

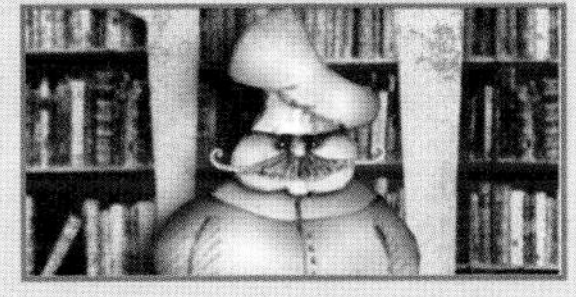

1 ☐ the baron's daughter **2** ☐ one of her aunts **3** ☐ the cook

d Who does the baron's daughter marry at the end of the story?

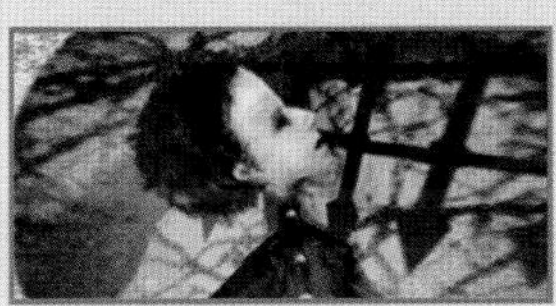

1 ☐ Herman von Starkenfaust **2** ☐ the Wild Hunter **3** ☐ Count von Altenburg

The Ghostly Bridegroom – Part 3

shock to give someone a very bad surprise; a very bad surprise

cheerful happy

The news of the count's death at the hands of robbers **shocked** everyone in the castle. The baron locked himself away in his room. His guests, who'd come to celebrate with him, couldn't think of leaving him now in his time of trouble. They walked around the castle or met in the hall in groups, talking and shaking their heads. And they ate and drank more than ever, to try and make themselves feel more **cheerful**.

But for the bride things were even worse. Just think of losing the man of your dreams before you've even taken him in your arms – and what a man he had been!

'The ghost of him was so polite and so fine-looking,' she said to herself. 'And I'm sure when he was alive, he was even politer and finer than that!'

She filled the castle with her moans and sighs.

On the second night after she'd met – and lost – the love of her life, she went to her room. One of her aunts – the fatter one – went with her. She didn't want the girl to sleep alone. This aunt, who was one of the best tellers of ghost stories in Germany, was telling one of her longest stories when she fell asleep in the middle of it.

The room looked out on a garden. Lying in bed, the young woman watched the moon shining on the leaves of the tree that stood outside her window. As she listened, the bell of the castle clock sounded twelve times. It was midnight!

Suddenly she heard soft guitar music coming from the garden. She left her bed and went to the window. A tall figure stood below, among the shadows of the trees. It looked up at her and just then, the silvery light of the moon shone down on it. She recognized the face. It was her ghostly bridegroom!

Suddenly she heard a loud scream in her ear, and her aunt – who'd woken up and followed her **niece** to the window – fell into her arms. When she looked down at the garden again, the ghost had disappeared.

It was now the aunt that needed the most looking after. She was really **terrified**. The young woman, on the other hand, felt that there was something even in the ghost of her lover that touched her heart. He seemed to her so manly. And – although the shadow of a man is not really enough to please a girl who's sick with love – a manly ghost is better than no

niece your sister's (or brother's) daughter

terrified very frightened

man at all.

The aunt said, 'I never want to sleep in this room again.'

The niece answered, 'And I'll never sleep in any other room in the castle except this one.'

So the niece decided to sleep in the room alone.

'Promise me faithfully you won't tell anyone about the ghost,' she asked her aunt.

'I promise,' the aunt replied.

The niece didn't want to lose the only happiness she had in the world. She didn't want to leave the room near that garden which her lover's ghost haunted at night.

I'm not sure if the aunt kept her promise or not. She loved telling stories, and it's fun to be the first person who learns about a piece of news and can then inform others. People say she kept her promise for over six days, but she didn't have to keep things secret for longer than that.

While she was sitting at the breakfast table on the seventh day, a servant came in, saying, 'Nobody can find the young lady. Her room's empty, she hasn't slept in her bed, and her window's open. She's gone!'

Everyone at the breakfast table was shocked at the news. Even the poorer relatives stopped eating for a moment. Then the fat aunt – who could say nothing when she first heard the news – suddenly began telling the story of what she'd seen in the garden, adding, 'The goblin's taken her!'

Two of the servants added, 'It's true! We heard a horse hurrying down the mountain road at about midnight. It was surely the ghostly bridegroom on his black horse, taking his bride away to the grave!'

All strongly believed what they said was true because awful things like this often happen in Germany, as you'll see if you read all the reports about them.

What a terrible thing to happen to the baron! Both as a father and as part of the great Katzenellenbogen family it was

unspeakably awful.

'Has a ghost taken my only daughter to the grave, or am I going to have a wild hunter as a son-in-law, or maybe half-goblin grandchildren?'

As usual he began running around worriedly and everyone in the castle became nervous.

He gave orders to his men, 'Take your horses and ride through the Odenwald forest at once. Look for my daughter on every hill, in every valley, and along every road.'

The baron himself had just pulled on his boots and was ready to get on his horse's back when he saw something that made him stop.

A young lady was riding towards the castle on a white horse, and a young man on a black horse was riding beside her.

She rode up to the gate and jumped down from the horse. At once she fell at the baron's feet and put her arms round his legs. It was his lost daughter, and her friend was – the ghostly bridegroom!

The baron was very surprised. He looked first at his daughter and then at the ghost and almost couldn't believe his eyes.

The ghost seemed in much better health since his visit to the land of the dead. His clothes were rich and fine, and he looked strong and manly in them. He was no longer white-faced and miserable. His face was pink and full of life, and happiness shone from his large brown eyes.

The mystery was at an end. The young man (as I'm sure you've guessed already) introduced himself to the baron as Herman von Starkenfaust.

He explained about his adventure with the young count, and told of how he'd hurried to the castle to bring the sad news, but that the baron had stopped him speaking again and again.

'When I saw the bride, she won my heart,' he went on, 'So I decided to stay for a while as the count in order to spend a few hours at her side.

'I was thinking about how I could say goodbye and go when suddenly your story about the goblin, Baron, gave me the idea for the strange way in which I left.

'Because you and my father are enemies, I knew later visits of mine wouldn't meet with your approval,' he added. 'So I came back in secret, haunting the garden below your daughter's window. There I met her, talked to her, won her heart, and carried her off with me to church where we've just celebrated our wedding.'

Normally the baron was a hard man. He liked his daughter to obey him, and his ancestors' enemies were his enemies, too. But he also loved his daughter, and he'd believed he would never see her again. Now he was happy to see her alive. And, although her husband was the son of his enemy, at least he wasn't a goblin!

'Young man,' he began, 'I have to say there's something not quite honest and true about the way you told me you were dead.'

But one of his friends, who was an old army man, said, 'Everything's fair in the name of love.'

Another old soldier added, 'Von Starkenfaust has recently been in the army, and what he's done needs to be seen in a different light because of that.'

So everything ended happily. The baron told his daughter and son-in-law there and then, 'I'm ready to forget what's happened and to welcome you both into my home with open arms.'

Everyone in the castle began celebrating again. The poor relatives made the young man's ears burn red with all the nice things they said to him:

'You're so brave.'

'You're so kind.'

'And so rich!'

The aunts, it was true, were a little shocked at the way their niece had forgotten so quickly everything that they'd tried to teach her.

'It was a serious mistake not to have metal **bars** put across her window,' said the thinner of the two, and her sister agreed.

The fatter aunt was very annoyed.

'I can't tell my wonderful story of the ghost in the garden any more,' she thought. 'Because the only ghost I've ever seen wasn't real after all.'

But the niece seemed very happy indeed to find out that her ghostly bridegroom was in fact a living husband in the end.

bars metal sticks that you put across windows to stop people climbing through them

ACTIVITIES

READING CHECK

1 Who says what in the story? Match the quotes with the people.

2 Correct the summary sentences.

a Everyone in the castle feels terrible when they hear about the ~~Wild Hunter~~. Count's death

b Late one night the bride sees her ghostly bridegroom in the bath.

c Six days later the servant disappears from her room.

d One of her aunts tells everyone that the baron has taken her away.

e Later that morning the bride returns to the castle with her new teacher.

f The ghostly doctor who came to visit her was really Herman von Starkenfaust.

g In the end, the baron is annoyed about his daughter's marriage.

ACTIVITIES

WORD WORK

1 Use the letters in the ghosts to make words from the story.

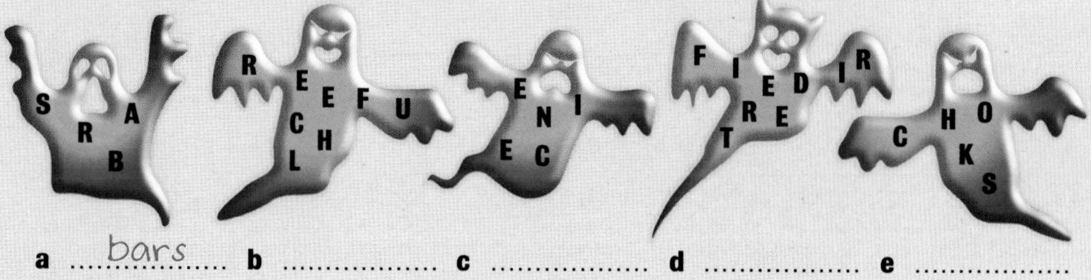

a ......bars...... **b** .... **c** .... **d** .... **e** ....

2 Replace two words in each sentence with a word from Activity 1.

a The aunts wanted to put ~~metal sticks~~ bars on the windows to stop anyone getting in or out.

b It was a bad surprise for everyone to hear about the count's funeral.

c The aunts looked after their brother's daughter after her mother died.

d You don't look very clearly happy! Has something bad happened?

e I'm really frightened of snakes. I faint when I see one.

GUESS WHAT

The next story is called *The Haunted Doll's House*. What do you think happens? Circle the words you think are correct.

a A man buys / finds / is given a beautiful old doll's house.

b At midnight the dolls in the doll's house start making noises / come to life / die.

c They show the man a story about a ghostly dog / a goblin / an old man dying.

The Haunted Doll's House – Part 1

by M. R. James

'Mr Chittenden, you must often get things like that in your shop,' said Mr Dillet, **pointing** with his stick to the doll's house in the window. Mr Dillet knew a lot about old things, and realized it was very special.

'You can't be serious,' replied Mr Chittenden. 'That should be in a museum.'

'You don't say!' laughed Mr Dillet. 'And how much is it?'

'Seventy-five pounds, sir.'

'That's a price for an American buyer. Let's say fifty.'

In the end they agreed on something in between, and half an hour later Mr Dillet took the thing away in his car.

Mr Chittenden stood at the shop door, smiling, with the money in his hand, and waved goodbye. Then he entered the back room where his wife was making tea.

'It's gone,' he said. 'Mr Dillet bought it.'

'Good!' said Mrs Chittenden. 'He needs a bit of a shock.'

'Well, I'm sure he's going to get it, and we won't have any more of it,' said Mr Chittenden, as they sat down to tea.

When Mr Dillet arrived home, Collins, the **butler**, came out to help him. Together they carried the doll's house up to Mr Dillet's bedroom and put it on his desk. Then Mr Dillet opened the front of it, and put everything in its place.

It was a beautiful example of an 18th century doll's house – six **feet** wide with a **chapel** on the left, and a **stable** on the right. The chapel had a bell and coloured glass windows. When the front of the house was open, you saw four large rooms inside: bedroom, kitchen, drawing room, and **dining room**, each with all the right furniture in it. The stable contained horses, a **coach**, and stable boys, and on top was the stable clock, also with a bell.

point to show something with a stick or a finger

butler the most important servant in a house

foot (*pl.* **feet**) 1 foot = 0.3048 metres

chapel a small church next to a big house; part of a big church

stable a building where horses live

dining room the room in a house where people eat

coach a kind of car with horses

The house stood on a **platform** which had steps going up to the front door, and a **terrace** on it. This platform also had a **drawer** in it, where you could keep different **curtains** and dolls' clothes, so you could change things when you wanted.

'It's wonderful,' sighed Mr Dillet. 'And what a low price! I could sell it in town for ten times more. It almost makes me afraid. I hope my luck doesn't change for the worse. But let's see who lives here.'

He put the dolls in a line in front of him. There was a **gentleman** and a lady in blue – he was in a suit and she in a fine dress. There were two children, a boy and a girl, together with a cook, a nurse, a servant, a coach driver, and three stable boys.

platform a high flat thing that something stands on

terrace a place near a house higher than the garden that you can walk along

drawer a thing like a box that you pull out from a piece of furniture

curtains people close these in front of windows at night to stop people looking in

gentleman a man from a good, usually rich family

four-poster an old bed with a roof on four posts and curtains around it

nightgown a long dress that men and women wore in bed

strike to make a bell in a clock sound the hour; to hit; to light a match

'Is there anyone more? Perhaps.' The **four-poster bed** had its curtains closed and he put his finger between them and felt inside. He pulled it out quickly because it seemed to him something there had felt almost alive. When he opened the curtains, he discovered an old gentleman with white hair in a long white **nightgown**, and put him with the others. That was all of them.

It was nearly dinner time, so in five minutes Mr Dillet put all the dolls back and went down for dinner. He didn't return to his own fine four-poster bed until eleven o'clock that night.

There was no **striking** clock in Mr Dillet's room, nor on the stairs or stables of his house, and none in the nearby church. But it was a clock striking that woke Mr Dillet from a pleasant sleep at one in the morning.

He was so surprised he sat up in bed.

Strangely, although the room was dark, he could see the doll's

house very clearly. It seemed that a full moon was shining down on it, and he could see trees around it – behind the chapel and the stable. It seemed too that he could smell the autumn smell of a cool September night. He thought he could hear horses moving in the stables. And with another shock he realized that above the roof, instead of the wall of his room, he was looking into a dark blue night sky.

He saw too that this was no four-roomed house with a movable front, but a real house with many rooms and stairs, although strangely smaller than it should be.

'You want to show me something,' he said to himself.

Two rooms in the doll's house were lit: one on the ground floor to the right of the door and one upstairs on the left. The first room was brightly lit, the second not so brightly. And he could see everything that was happening inside those rooms. The first room was the dining room. Dinner was finished, but glasses and **wine** were still on the table. The gentleman and lady in blue sat alone there. They were talking seriously, and from time to time it seemed they stopped to listen. Once the gentleman got up, opened the window, put his head out and put his hand to his ear. Then he went from the window and from the room and the woman was left standing alone there, holding a **candle**. Looking at her face, it seemed that she was fighting against a strong fear inside her, and that she was winning. She had an unpleasant face, too: wide, flat and too clever for its own good.

Now the gentleman came back into the room and she took something from his hand and hurried out. He too disappeared, but only for a moment. The front door slowly opened and he came out and stood on the terrace. Then he turned to the upstairs window which was lit, and shook his closed hand angrily up at it.

It was time to look at that upper window. Through it you could see a four-poster bed, and a nurse sleeping in an armchair

wine a red or white alcoholic drink made from grapes

candle it burns and gives light; in the past people used them to see at night

by the fire. In the bed an old man lay awake, and – from the way he moved his hands on the bed covers – he was worried. Beyond the bed, the door opened. The lady in blue came in with the candle. She put it down and woke up the nurse. She had an open bottle of wine in her hand. The nurse took it and put some wine into a pan. She added sugar and **spices** from little pots, and then put the pan on the fire to cook.

At the same time, the old man seemed to call weakly to the lady. She went to him, felt his wrist, and bit her lip. The old man looked at her worriedly and pointed to the window. She went to the window and then, as the gentleman had done, she opened it, put her head out – with her hand to her ear – and listened. Then she pulled her head in and shook it at the old man, who seemed to sigh.

Now the spiced wine was ready. The nurse put it in a silver bowl and took it to the old man. He waved it away, but the lady and the nurse moved closer, probably asking him to drink. In the end it's clear he said 'yes', because they helped him to sit up and put the bowl to his lips. He drank most of it, then lay down. The lady smiled goodnight, and left the room. She took the candle, the bottle, the bowl, and the pan with her. The nurse went back to her chair and for a time everything was quiet.

Suddenly the old man sat up in bed and opened his mouth wide. He was probably crying out, because the nurse jumped up and ran to the bedside. The old man looked terrible. His face was dark red, almost black, his round eyes were staring, both hands pulled at his chest, and his lips were white.

For a moment the nurse left him, ran to the door, and threw it open, clearly calling for help: then she ran back and tried nervously to calm him down. But as the lady, her husband, and several servants hurried with shocked faces into the room, the old man fell back on the bed, his arms stopped moving and his pained face slowly became calm and still.

spice something that you put in food or drink to make it taste nice

A few moments later, lights showed to the left of the house, and a lit coach drove up to the front door.

A man in black with white hair got out and ran up the front steps, carrying a black bag. He was met at the door by the man and wife. She seemed to be crying and he had a long sad face. They took their visitor into the dining room, where he put his bag of papers on the table. Then he listened with a worried face to what they told him. He seemed to say no to an invitation to have something to eat or drink, returned to his coach, and drove off the way he'd come. As the gentleman in blue watched him from the top of the steps, an unpleasant smile covered his fat white face. Then all became dark as the coach disappeared into the night.

ACTIVITIES

READING CHECK

Are these sentences about the first part of *The Haunted Doll's House* true or false? Tick the boxes.

		True	False
a	Mr Dillet is very happy with the doll's house when he takes it home.	☑	☐
b	He keeps it in his bedroom.	☐	☐
c	He is woken in the night by the church clock near his house.	☐	☐
d	Mr Dillet sees a man and woman in the dining room of the house.	☐	☐
e	The gentleman looks frightened of something.	☐	☐
f	The lady in blue takes some wine to an old man.	☐	☐
g	The nurse tries to help the old man, but he dies.	☐	☐
h	A man in black arrives at the house and visits the old man.	☐	☐

WORD WORK

1 Correct the underlined words in Mr Dillet's diary with the words in the box.

pointed	nightgown	~~strike~~	wine	candle	spices	drawer	gentleman

Wednesday 16th October

I woke when I heard a clock ~~touch~~ (strike) one o'clock. Strangely the doll's house looked like a real house, and I could see light in two of its rooms. A lady and <u>boy</u> in blue were in the dining room. They were drinking <u>coffee</u> by the light of a <u>fire</u>. The man <u>waved</u> at the window with his hand, then stood up and left the room. In a room upstairs I watched a nurse mix some <u>rice</u> into a drink for an old man. He was sitting up in bed in a <u>suit</u>. There was a <u>cupboard</u> in the small table next to the old man's bed. Perhaps there were some important papers in it?

2 Complete the words to label the picture of the doll's house below.

a chapel

b _ oa _ _

c _ ou _ - _ o _ _ e _

d _ e _ _ a _ e

e _ u _ _ ai _ _

f _ u _ _ e r

g _ i _ i _ _ _ oo _

h _ _ a _ _ e

i _ _ a _ _ o _ _

GUESS WHAT

What do you think happens at the end of the story? Tick two boxes.

a ☐ The old man's ghost visits the doll's house family and something terrible happens.

b ☐ Mr Dillet takes the doll's house back to the shop where he bought it.

c ☐ Mr Dillet meets the maker of the doll's house and learns the family's true story.

d ☐ Mr Dillet visits the village where the real house stood and hears a clock striking.

The Haunted Doll's House – Part 2

All was dark in Mr Dillet's bedroom, but he stayed sitting up in his bed. He guessed he would see more.

The front of the doll's house began to shine again, but the lights were now in different places. One was at the top of the house and the other in the chapel. There was a **coffin** in the middle of the chapel with four candles in tall silver holders around it. A black **cloth** lay over the coffin and, as he watched, the cloth seemed to move up at one end and fell to the floor, leaving the coffin uncovered. One of the candles fell to the floor also.

Now Mr Dillet looked at the room at the top of the house. A boy and girl lay in two small beds and there was a four-poster bed for the nurse. She wasn't there, but the father and mother were. They were dressed in black clothes, but were laughing and talking with each other and with the children. Then, unnoticed by the children, the father left the room, taking a long white nightgown from by the door as he went. He shut the door behind him. A few moments later, the door opened slowly and a large terrible white thing entered and moved towards the beds.

Then the figure suddenly stopped, lifted up its arms, and showed itself to be – the laughing father, of course! The children were terrified – the boy hid under the bed covers and the girl ran to her mother's arms. The parents tried to calm them down, took them on their knees, and showed them that the old nightgown couldn't hurt them. At last they put the children to bed, waving to them as they left the room. As they left, the nurse came in, and soon the light in the children's room at the top of the house went out.

Mr Dillet stayed watching without moving.

Then a new kind of light, not a candle, but something unpleasant and cold shone into the room at the top of the

coffin a wooden or metal box that you put a dead person's body in

cloth clothes are made of this

house as the door opened again. Something very frightening entered the room. The watcher couldn't describe it beyond saying it looked like a **frog** as big as a man with thin white hair on top. It went to the little beds and was busy over them for a while, but not for long.

The noise of weak little cries, sounding very far off but still awful, reached the listener's ear. Suddenly the house was full of lights moving, figures running, doors opening and closing. The clock in the stable sounded one, and darkness came.

Then, for the last time, the house shone brightly again. At the foot of the steps by the front door two lines of black figures waited, holding burning lights. More dark figures came down the steps, carrying two little coffins. And the lines of dark figures carrying lights, with the coffins between them, moved to the chapel on the left.

The hours of night passed very slowly, thought Mr Dillet. He slowly moved from sitting to lying in his bed, but he didn't close an eye. Early next morning he sent for the doctor.

The doctor found him uneasy and nervous, and said that sea air was the answer. So Mr Dillet was driven slowly to a quiet place on the east coast.

One of the first people he met as he walked along by the sea was Mr Chittenden, who had also been told to take his wife away for a change of air.

'I'm a little **upset** with you,' said Mr Dillet.

'I'm not surprised, sir. My wife and I went through a lot ourselves. But what could I do? I couldn't throw the thing away – it was a really nice piece. And I couldn't really tell a buyer, "I'm selling you a haunted doll's house which will always come to life at one o'clock in the morning." I didn't want people to think me and my wife were crazy.'

'Will you buy it back from me?'

'No thanks! I'll tell you what, though. I'll pay you back what you gave for it, except the ten pounds I paid, of course.

frog a small green animal that lives near water and has long back legs for jumping

upset unhappy; to make someone feel unhappy

And you can do what you want with it.'

Later in the day the two men had another whispered conversation in the smokers' room at their hotel.

'Tell me, how much do you know about that thing, and where it came from?'

'Honestly, Mr Dillet, I don't know the house. Of course it came out of an old country house, that's clear. I've got a feeling it was from somewhere not far from this place. The man I bought it from isn't one who usually sells to me, and I haven't seen him since then. But this was his part of the country. And that's all I can say about it.

'But, Mr Dillet, I've got a question. The old man who drives up to the door – you've seen him, haven't you? Ah yes, I thought so. Do you think he was the doctor or the **lawyer**? My wife says the doctor, but I say the lawyer because of all the papers in his bag, and the one he took out last but didn't open.'

'I agree,' said Mr Dillet. 'I think that was the old man's **will**, ready for him to write his name at the bottom.'

'I thought the same,' replied Mr Chittenden. 'Probably a will that didn't leave any of the old man's money to the younger ones. But it's taught me something. I won't buy any doll's houses again, or spend time and money at the cinema. And about the idea of **poisoning** grandad, well, I couldn't do it. I prefer to live happily with my relatives – always have done, always will do.'

The next day Mr Dillet went to the town museum. He wanted to try and find the house at the heart of the mystery. He looked at lots of old pictures of houses on the walls, but couldn't see his house among them. He looked through lots of old **church records** but again he had no luck. Then, in an almost empty room, he saw an old **model** of a church which made his heart grow suddenly cold. It looked like more work by the same man who had made his doll's house. He read the small notice in front of it carefully.

This model of Saint Stephen's Church, Coxham,
was given to the museum by Mr J Merewether
of Ilbridge House in 1877.
It is the work of his ancestor, James Merewether, 1786.

He went back to look at a map of the country nearby that he'd noticed earlier on the wall. There he saw that Ilbridge house was in the village of Coxham. Then he went back to the old

lawyer someone who helps people with papers that tell them what they must do or musn't do

will the paper that says which people you want to have your money when you die

poison to give people something that kills them when they eat or drink it

church records books belonging to a church that contain lists of people's weddings and funerals

model a little building that someone makes to put on show

church records and soon found the funeral of Roger Milford, aged 76, on the 11th of September 1757, and of Roger and Elizabeth Merewether, aged 9 and 7, on the 19th of the same month. Although he wasn't sure this was the family, it seemed worth visiting Coxham, and so he drove there that afternoon.

In the north of the church there was a Milford chapel. In it there was a stone to the memory of Roger Milford: 'Father, and successful lawyer'. 'This stone was put here by his loving daughter Elizabeth, who died soon after losing her caring father and her dear children,' it said. The last words had obviously been added later.

In the chapel too, a later stone spoke of, 'James Merewether, husband of Elizabeth, who – when a young man – was a promising architect, but who stopped this work on the death of his wife and children, and who ended his days in a comfortable **retirement home**.'

The children had smaller, less grandly-worded stones. They'd both died on the night of the 12th of September.

Mr Dillet felt sure that in Ilbridge House he'd found the place where it had all happened. In some old picture some day perhaps he'll find he's right. But the Ilbridge House of today is not the house he was looking for. It's a newer red-stone house which was built in the 1840s.

Not far from the new house, in a lower part of the garden, near some old trees, is a terraced platform covered with grass. That, someone told Mr Dillet, was the place where the old house had once stood.

As he drove out of the village, the church clock sounded four, and Mr Dillet put his hands over his ears. It was not the first time that he'd heard that bell.

These days, waiting for an American buyer, the doll's house rests, carefully covered, in the upstairs room over Mr Dillet's stables. It was taken there by his butler on the day that he left for the seaside.

retirement home a place where people go to live when they are old, or needing special care

ACTIVITIES

READING CHECK

Complete the gaps in these sentences about Part 2 of the story.

a First of all Mr Dillet sees something happen in the chapel .
b The children are terrified of their ________ pretending to be a ________ .
c Something frightening goes to the ________ room and ________ them.
d After he speaks to his doctor, Mr Dillet goes away to the ________ because he is ________ .
e He meets Mr Chittenden and ________ there.
f They all think that the ________ and ________ killed the granddad.
g The man who made the doll's house also made a model ________ , now in the town museum.
h Mr Dillet visits the ________ where the Merewether family lived.
i He sees the ________ of the whole family in Coxham.
j Elizabeth Merewether died soon after her ________ , Roger Milford, and her ________ , Roger and Elizabeth.
k When ________ leaves Coxham he recognises the sound of the ________ .

WORD WORK

Use the words in the coach and horses picture to answer the questions on page 53.

a Which small animal has four legs and can live in water and on land?
A ....frog.......

b Where do old people live when they have no family to take care of them?
In a ....

c Where do we put a dead body before it is buried? In a ....

d A How do you think that Lucrezia Borgia killed her enemies?
B Did she .... them?

e What's that little building on your desk? A .... of the Taj Mahal.

f Where can you find out about the history of an English family?
In ....

g How do you feel when something bad happens to you? ....

h What do people put on a dinner table before they put plates and glasses on it?
A ....

i Which person helps you when you have problems with the police? A ....

j Where do you write who will get your money when you die? In your ....

GUESS WHAT

Match the phrases with the two main characters in *Man-size in Marble*. Use a dictionary to help you.

a painter
a writer
poor
hates cooking and cleaning
loves listening to old stories
nervous
doesn't believe in ghosts
believes in ghosts
musical
kind

Man-size in Marble – Part 1

by E. Nesbit

My name is Jack Collis, and every word of this story is true – although many people probably won't believe it. These days people need a **logical** explanation before they believe anything. If you want an explanation like that, perhaps my wife Laura and I just **imagined** everything that happened to us on that 31st of October 1893. I'll let you, the reader, decide.

When I became engaged to Laura, we knew we wouldn't have much money when we married. I used to **paint** in those days, and Laura wrote. Living in town was expensive, so we started looking for a country **cottage** – something pretty but with an inside toilet – to live in after we were married. We searched in newspaper **advertisements** for some time, but all the cottages that we visited with inside toilets looked terrible, and all the pretty ones had no inside toilets.

On our wedding day we were still homeless, but on our **honeymoon** we found the **perfect** place. It was in Brenzett, a little village on a hill in the south, not far from the coast. We'd gone there from the seaside town where we were staying to visit the church. Nearby we found a pretty cottage with a bathroom, standing all alone about two miles from the village. It was a long low building with flowers round it, all that was left of a big old house which had once stood here. We decided to rent it at once. It was awfully cheap.

We spent the rest of our honeymoon buying old furniture from shops in the nearby market town, and new curtains and chair covers from one of the big shops up in London, and the place soon began to feel like home. It was easy to work there. I never got tired of painting the countryside and the wonderful sky I could see through the open window, and Laura sat at the table and wrote about all of it, and about me.

logical that you can understand by using your head, not your heart

imagine to see pictures in your head

paint to put different colours on paper to make a picture

cottage a small house in the country

advertisement you pay to put this information in a newspaper

honeymoon a holiday that two people take together just after they get married

perfect with nothing wrong

We found a tall old woman from the village to cook and clean for us. She was tidy, skilled at cooking, and understood everything about gardens. She also told us the old names of the places nearby, and **tales** of robbers who'd once lived there, and of ghosts who sometimes met people in the neighbourhood when it was late at night.

She was the perfect servant for us. Laura hated cooking and cleaning, and I loved listening to old stories. So we left Mrs Dorman to manage the cottage, and used her old tales in stories with pictures that we sent to magazines, which helped to bring in some money.

We had three months of married happiness, and never argued. Then one October evening I went to visit our only neighbour, Dr Kelly – a pleasant Irishman – for a talk and a smoke of my **pipe**. I left Laura all smiles, writing a funny magazine story about village life. But when I came back, I found her sitting on the window seat, crying.

'What's the matter?' I asked.

'Oh, Jack! It's Mrs Dorman,' she moaned. 'She says she has

tale story

pipe something you use for smoking with a long stick and a small bowl at one end

path a narrow road for people to walk on

churchyard a place next to a church where dead people are put under the ground

marble fine white or grey stone

tomb where people put a dead person in a building

to go before the end of the month to care for her sick niece. But I don't believe her because her niece is always ill. I think someone's turned her against us. She seemed so strange when she spoke to me.'

'Don't worry, dearest,' I said.

'But don't you see? If she leaves, none of the other villagers will want to come here, and I'll have to cook and wash plates and you'll have to clean knives and forks and we won't have time for writing or painting.'

'I'll speak to Mrs Dorman when she comes back,' I said, trying to calm her down. 'Perhaps she wants more money. It'll be all right. Let's walk up to the church.'

The church was large and lovely, and we enjoyed going there on nights when the moon was full. The **path** to it went through a wood, past two fields, and round the **churchyard** wall. It had been the old way they used to take coffins to the church for funerals.

There were lots of dark trees in the churchyard. The church door was a heavy wooden one, and the windows were of coloured glass. Inside there were rows of dark wooden seats, and at the eastern end there were two grey **marble** figures of old knights in armour, one on each side, lying on their **tombs**.

Strangely you could always see them, even if the rest of the church was nearly in darkness.

Their names were lost in the past, but the villagers said they'd been wild and terrible men, and that one night, in a great storm, **lightning** had struck their big old house and destroyed it. Interestingly this was the place where now our cottage stood. For all that, their sons' gold had bought them the place in the church where they were buried.

Looking at their hard, proud marble faces, it was easy to believe the story was true.

The church looked at its best and strangest that evening. We sat down together without speaking, and stared for a time at the fine stone walls around us. We walked over to look at the sleeping knights. Then we went out and rested on the seat by the church door, looking across the fields while the sun went down. As we came away, we felt that even doing the cooking and cleaning ourselves wasn't really so bad.

When we arrived home, Mrs Dorman had come back from the village. I asked her to come into my painting room for a short talk.

'Mrs Dorman,' I said, when we were alone, 'Aren't you happy here with us?'

'Oh, no, sir. You and your dear lady have always been most kind to me.'

'Aren't we paying you enough?'

'No, sir. I get quite enough.'

'Then why don't you want to stay with us?'

'My niece is ill,' she said uneasily. 'I must leave before the end of the month.'

'But your niece has been ill since we arrived.'

A long uncomfortable silence followed. I broke it.

'Can't you stay for another week?'

'No, sir. I must go by Thursday. But perhaps I can come back to you next week.'

lightning a line of bright light which comes down quickly from the sky in a storm and can burn things that it hits

I was now sure all she wanted was a short holiday.

'But why must you leave *this* week?' I asked.

She looked nervous and went on slowly.

'They say, sir, that this was a big house in the old days, and that many strange, dark things happened here. The owners, when young men, loved nothing better than attacking, robbing, and killing both men and women on land and sea. They were dangerous men, sir, and no one stood up against them. So, year by year, they went from bad to worse. In the end their terrible crimes against nature, and all the deaths of the poor little children from the villages nearby, brought the lightning down from the sky to destroy them.'

I was pleased that Laura wasn't in the room with us. She was always nervous, and I felt that these old stories would perhaps make our house less dear to her.

'Tell me more, Mrs Dorman,' I said. 'Please. I'm not like lots of young people these days who laugh at strange things like that.'

This was true in a way. I loved her stories, although I didn't really believe them.

'Well, sir,' she began in a low voice, 'Perhaps you've seen the two figures in the church.'

'You mean the knights,' I said cheerfully.

'I mean those two bodies **man-size** in marble. They say that at **Halloween** those two bodies sit up and get off their

man-size as big as a man

Halloween the night of 31 October

tombs, and that – as the church clock strikes eleven – they walk in their marble out of the church door, over the graves, and along the path.'

'And where do they go?' I asked interestedly.

'They come back here to their house, sir, and if anyone meets them ...'

'Well, what happens?' I asked.

But I couldn't get another word from her, although she warned me, 'Lock the house early on Halloween, sir, and make the **sign** of the **cross** over the door and windows.'

'But who was here at Halloween last year?'

'No one, sir. The lady who owned the house only stayed in the summer and always went to London a full month before the night. I'm sorry to bring trouble to you and your lady, but my niece is ill and I must go on Thursday.'

She'd decided she would go, and that nothing we could say would stop her.

I didn't tell Laura the tale of the figures that 'walked in their marble'. I didn't want to upset her. This was, I felt, different from Mrs Dorman's other stories – and I didn't want to talk about it until the day was past.

I was painting a picture of Laura in front of the window all that week, and while I worked on it, I couldn't stop thinking about the tale of the two knights.

On Thursday Mrs Dorman left, saying to Laura as she went, 'Don't go out too much, madam, and if there's anything I can do for you next week, I'll be happy to help.'

From that I understood she wished to come back after Halloween, though to the end she continued with the story of her sick niece.

Thursday went well. Laura cooked a lovely dinner, and I washed the knives, forks and plates not too badly afterwards. Soon Friday came, and it's what happened then that this story is really about.

sign a shape that you make with your fingers in the air

cross a Christian sign where two lines meet, like this †

ACTIVITIES

READING CHECK

Choose the right phrases to complete the sentences. Tick the correct box.

a Laura and Jack decide to rent the cottage because . . .
- **1** it's near the sea. ☐
- **2** they find it when they are on their honeymoon. ☐
- **3** they don't have a lot of money. ☑

b For the first three months in the cottage . . .
- **1** they both work and are very happy. ☐
- **2** Laura does all the cooking and cleaning. ☐
- **3** they are afraid of ghosts haunting the place. ☐

c Mrs Dorman, the servant, wants to stop working for them because . . .
- **1** she doesn't want to be near the house at Halloween. ☐
- **2** her niece is sick. ☐
- **3** she wants a short holiday. ☐

d Mrs Dorman tells Jack a story about . . .
- **1** some robbers who always visit the house at Halloween. ☐
- **2** the ghosts of the knights whose tombs are in the church. ☐
- **3** the ghosts of some dead children from the nearby villages. ☐

e Jack decides . . .
- **1** to tell Laura the story about the knights. ☐
- **2** to leave the cottage until after Halloween. ☐
- **3** not to tell Laura the story about the knights. ☐

WORD WORK

1 Complete the sentences on page 61 with the words in the picture.

honeymoon
sign
imagine
perfect
~~logical~~
paint
tale
man-size

a He's a ....logical.... man. He thinks before he does anything.

b Just after they were married they went off on their .... to Malta.

c My grandmother made a .... with her hand for me to come closer.

d When did Leonardo da Vinci .... the Mona Lisa?

e Do you know the old .... of how Arthur became the king of England?

f There was a .... white figure in the snowy garden.

g Can you .... a world with no very rich or very poor people in it?

h Your teeth are .... There's nothing wrong with them.

2 Circle new words from the story in the wordsquare. Label the pictures with them.

GUESS WHAT

What do you think happens on the night of Halloween? Tick the correct box.

	Yes	No
a Mrs Dorman returns with surprising news.	☐	☐
b Jack goes to the church in the evening and something terrible happens.	☐	☐
c Dr Kelly is killed on his way to visit a patient.	☐	☐
d The marble knights leave the church.	☐	☐
e Laura is found dead in the cottage.	☐	☐

Man-size in Marble – Part 2

Everything that happened on that day is burned into my memory, and I'll tell the story as clearly as I can.

I got up early, I remember, and had just managed to light the kitchen fire when my lovely wife came running downstairs as bright as that clear October morning. We enjoyed making breakfast together, and washing the plates and knives afterwards. We cleaned and tidied all morning, and then had cold meat and coffee for lunch. Laura seemed, if possible, even sweeter than usual and the walk that we took together that afternoon was the happiest time of my life. When we'd watched the sun go down, and the evening **mist** thicken in the fields, we came back to the house, silently, hand in hand.

'You're sad, dearest,' I said as we sat down together in our little sitting room.

'Yes, I am,' she replied, 'Or a little uneasy. I don't think I'm very well. I've **shivered** two or three times since we came in, and it isn't cold in here, is it?'

'You haven't caught a cold from the mist, have you?' I asked her worriedly.

'I don't think so,' she said. Then she added suddenly, 'Jack, do you ever feel something **evil**'s going to happen?'

'No,' I smiled. 'I don't believe in that kind of thing.'

'I do,' she went on. 'The night my father died I knew it, although he was far away in the north of Scotland.'

We sat watching the fire for some time in silence. In the end she jumped up and kissed me suddenly.

'Don't worry about me,' she said. 'I'm better now. What a baby I am! Let's play some music together.'

So we spent a happy hour or two at the **piano**.

At about half past ten I felt I needed my pipe. Laura looked so white I felt it would be awful to smoke inside, so I said, 'I'll take my pipe outside.'

mist a thin cloud near the ground

shiver when your body repeatedly moves a little from fear or the cold

evil very bad

piano a big musical instrument that you play by pressing black and white keys

'I'll come too.'

'Not tonight, dearest. Go to bed. You look really tired.'

I kissed her, and was turning to go when she threw her arms round my neck, and held me close, saying, 'I never want to let you go. Don't stay out too long.'

'I won't.'

I walked slowly out of the front door, leaving it unlocked. What a night it was! The sky was full of dark clouds hurrying by, and a thin mist covered the stars. The moon swam high up, sometimes disappearing behind the fast-moving cloud river, and sometimes shining down on the trees which waved slowly and noiselessly below. There was a strange grey light that night which shone over all the earth.

I walked up and down. Everything was silent. The wind was so high in the sky even the dead leaves on the path were still and quiet. Across the fields I could see the church tower standing black against the sky. I heard the church bell striking. It was eleven o'clock already.

I turned to go into the cottage, but the night held me. I couldn't go back into our warm rooms just yet. I decided to walk over to the church. I felt in a strange way I should offer up my thanks there for my faithful, loving wife. I imagined then our long, sweet life together.

As I walked slowly along the edge of the wood a sound from among the trees broke the stillness of the night. I could clearly hear **footsteps** that **echoed** mine. 'It's probably a villager looking for fallen branches for their fire, or hoping to catch some forest animal under cover of darkness,' I thought. 'But he really should learn to step more lightly.'

I turned into the wood. Now the footsteps seemed to come from the path behind me. 'It must be an echo,' I said to myself.

Soon I was crossing the churchyard. I stopped for a while at the seat where Laura and I had watched the sun go down. Then I saw the church door was open. I felt bad about not

footsteps the noise people make with their feet when they walk

echo to make the same sound; when a sound hits something and comes back to the listener

closing it well on our last visit, for we were the only people who came there except on Sundays. Then, suddenly, I remembered this was the day and the hour when the villagers believed 'the shapes in man-size marble' began to walk.

I knew I had to go into the church. I planned to tell Mrs Dorman I'd seen the knights there at eleven o'clock on Halloween and that her tale was just a crazy story, nothing more. When I walked inside, everything was in darkness.

As I went towards the eastern end of the church it seemed strangely larger. Then the moon came out and showed me the reason. The man-size marble bodies were gone!

Was I going crazy? I went forward and put my hand out to touch the flat tops of the tombs. Had someone stolen them? A sudden nameless fear filled my heart, and I shivered. Something unbelievably evil was going to happen, I knew. I ran from the church, biting my lip to stop myself from screaming.

I hurried across the fields towards the light that shone from our cottage window. Suddenly a black figure jumped out of the blackness in front of me. I ran towards it crazily, shouting, 'Get out of my way!'

But a hand took my arm and held it strongly. The big Irish doctor shook me repeatedly.

'Hey, there,' he cried.

'Let me go,' I shouted. 'You don't understand! The marble figures have gone from the church!'

He laughed long and loud at that. 'You've been listening to too many old village tales,' he said.

'I've seen the empty tombs, I tell you,'

'Look, come with me. I'm going over to old Palmer's. His daughter's ill. We can stop at the church on the way and you can show me what you think you saw.'

'All right,' I said.

He still held my arm as we entered the church and walked to the eastern end of it. I had my eyes closed. I knew that the figures wouldn't be there.

I heard Kelly strike a match.

'Here they are,' said the doctor. 'As large as life.'

I opened my eyes and by the light of Kelly's match I saw the two shapes lying 'in their marble' on the tombs.

'Thank you,' I said. 'Perhaps it was a **trick** of the light, or perhaps I've been working too hard. I can't understand it. I was sure they were gone.'

'I know. Just don't let your **thoughts** run away with you.'

He was looking closely at the figure on the right, whose stony face was the most evil and deadly.

trick a thing which makes people think something is true

thought something that you think

'Will you look at that!' he said, pointing. 'The hand on this one's broken.'

He was right, but I was sure that the last time Laura and I had been there it had been perfect.

'Perhaps someone was trying to steal them,' he said calmly.

'That still doesn't explain what I thought I saw.'

'Too much painting and too much of your old pipe explains that,' he laughed.

'Let's go,' I said, feeling a little better. 'My wife will be worried. Come and have a glass of **whisky** with me. We'll drink to logical explanations, and **to hell with** ghosts.'

'All right. It's late. I'll go to old Palmer's in the morning,' he replied. Perhaps he thought that I needed his help more than Palmer's daughter.

whisky a strong alcoholic drink that is made in Scotland

to hell with we say this when we think something is stupid or we don't care about it

So, talking of different explanations for ghosts, we walked back to our cottage. As we came nearer I saw the light shining out of the front door. The sitting room door was open, too. Had Laura gone out?

'Come in,' I said, and Dr Kelly followed me into the sitting room. It was brightly lit by candles all over the place. Light, I remembered, was Laura's answer to nervousness. Poor girl, I thought. I'd been so stupid to leave her. But where was she?

Then I turned to the open window and saw her. Had she gone there to watch for me? And what had come into the room behind her? To what had she turned with her face full of **horror**? My poor wife! Had she thought it was my footsteps she'd heard as she turned to meet – what?

horror a feeling of great fear or shock

She'd fallen back across a table by the window, and her body lay half on it and half on the window seat. Her head was thrown back, her long untied hair was touching the carpet. Her lips were pulled back from her teeth and her eyes were wide open in fear. They saw nothing now. What had they seen last?

The doctor moved towards her, but I pushed him to one side and ran to her, crying, 'It's all right, Laura. You're safe now.'

Her soft body fell against mine. I held her and kissed her, calling her dear name again and again, but I think I knew already that she was dead.

Both her hands were closed. In one of them she held something very strongly. When I was quite sure she was dead, and that nothing mattered any more, I let Doctor Kelly open that hand to see what it held.

It was a grey marble finger.

ACTIVITIES

READING CHECK

1 Put these phrases into the correct places in the summary.

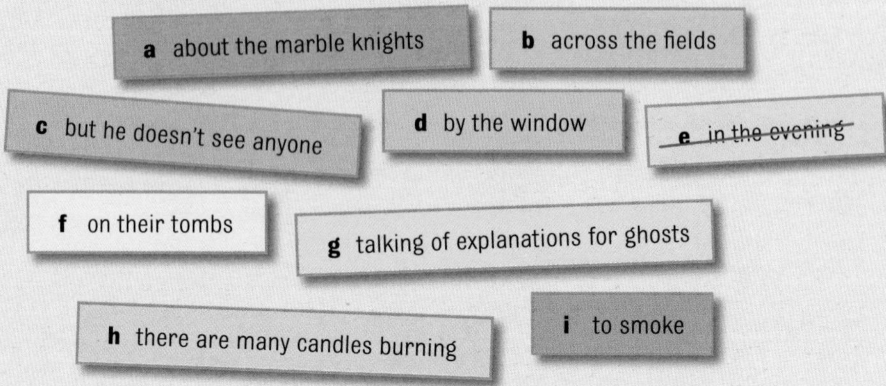

Jack and Laura spend the day together happily, working in the house and having a walk ..... When they get back to the cottage, Laura is nervous and has a feeling that something bad is going to happen. They play some music together and then Jack goes outside ..... It's a beautiful night and he decides to walk to the church. On the way there he hears the noise of people walking in the wood and on the path ..... When he reaches the church, he sees the door open and remembers Mrs Dorman's story ..... He walks in and is terrified to see that the knights aren't on their tombs. He runs wildly ..... to the cottage, but a black figure jumps out in front of him. It is Dr Kelly. Jack tells him what he has seen, but when they return to the church together, the knights are there ..... Dr Kelly notices that one of them has a missing finger. The two men walk back to the cottage together ..... When they reach the cottage, the door is open, ..., and Laura is lying across a table ..... She is dead, and in her hand she's holding a grey marble finger.

WORD WORK

Find words in the pipe smoke, match them with the sentences, and show where they go.

If you shout in here, you'll hear an come back to you.
.....echo.....

That man is an criminal.
....

He started running when he heard behind him.
....

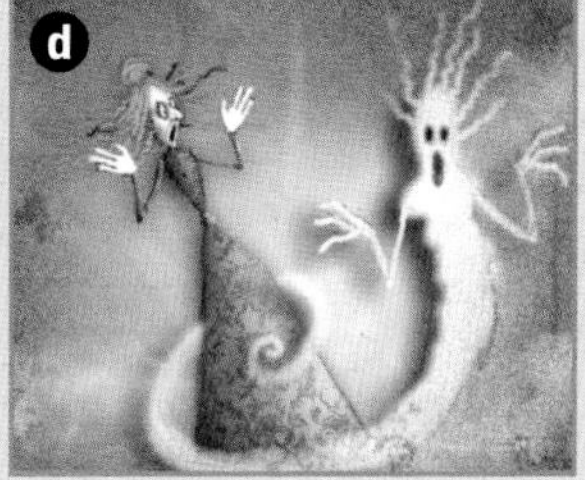

Imagine my when I saw the ghost! ....

There's a lot of over the mountains this morning.
....

I'm because it's so cold! Let's have a hot drink.
....

Can you show me a card?
....

PROJECT A Expanding texts

1 Match the passages with the stories they come from.

The Faithful Ghost ☐ Meeting Mrs Dumoise ☐ The Ghostly Bridegroom ☐
The Haunted Doll's House ☐ Man-size in Marble ☐

a The mysterious bridegroom listened to this story with great interest. Just before the baron finished, the handsome young man began to stand up.

b *He passed through me suddenly and, giving a terrible long low moan of great sadness, he disappeared quickly out of the narrow window by the back stairs.*

c *We sat down quietly together without speaking, and stared thoughtfully for a time at the fine thick stone walls around us. We walked slowly over to look at the sleeping knights.*

d *The poor old man looked terrible. His face was dark red, almost black, his large round eyes were staring in fear, both hands pulled repeatedly at his chest, and his thin lips were white.*

e The sun had gone down behind the dark mountains, and it was very windy. Dumoise stood silently in front of the old house, waiting for the useless man to come back.

2 Find the same passages in the stories. Compare them, and highlight the extra words in the passages above.

3 Add the extra words to the passage from Man-size in Marble in the correct place. Mark exactly where they go like this: ⋀ The words are in order.

and thoughtfully	wild	purple	silver	full	for a few seconds		
leafless	calmly	perfectly	autumn	garden	empty	silent	heavily

I walked slowly out of the front door, leaving it unlocked. What a night it was! The sky was full of dark clouds hurrying by, and a thin mist covered the stars. The moon swam high up, sometimes disappearing behind the fast-moving cloud river, and sometimes shining down on the trees which waved slowly and noiselessly below. There was a strange grey light that night which shone over all the earth.

I walked up and down. Everything was silent. The wind was so high in the sky that even the dead leaves on the path were still and quiet. Across the fields I could see the church tower standing black against the sky. I heard the church bell striking. It was eleven o'clock already.

4 Choose a passage of 8–10 lines from one of the stories. Copy it out and add 8–10 extra words or phrases.

5 Swap passages with a partner. Read and highlight the new words.

PROJECT B Haunted homes

1 Read about a haunted home and answer the questions.

a Where is the building and what is it used for?

b By which two names is the ghost known?

c What is known about her past?

d What kind of things does she do?

e What does she look like?

f How do people feel about her?

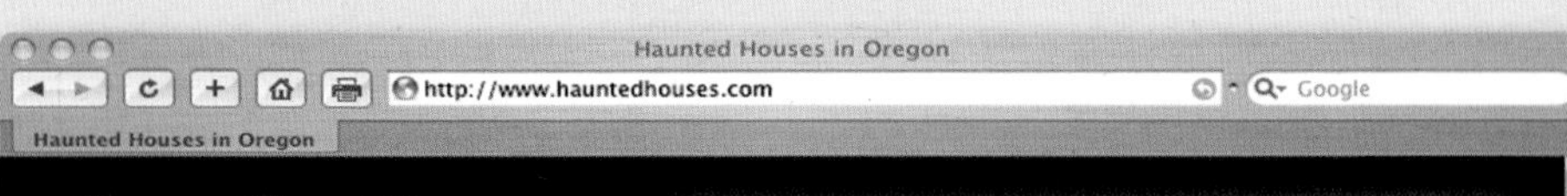

Heceta House

Location: Florence, Oregon, USA

The Heceta Head Lighthouse, built in 1894, was named after a Spanish sailor who reached Oregon in the 18th century. It is a working lighthouse, and its light shines 45 kilometres out to sea.

Heceta House – where the Lighthouse Keepers used to live – is now a small hotel. People say it is haunted by the ghost of a 'Grey Lady'. It is thought that she was the wife of a past lighthouse keeper, and the mother of a young child whose grave is near the lighthouse. Also known as 'Rue', the ghost is said to move objects, open and close drawers and cupboard doors and do other strange things.

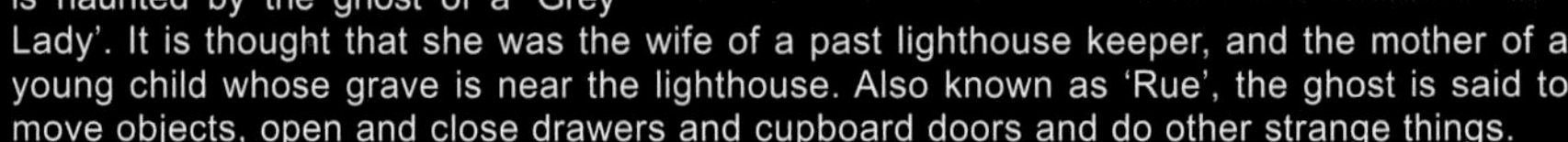

In the 1970s a workman came face to face with Rue in an attic room and ran downstairs terrified. He described her as a woman with silver hair in a long, dark dress. Some days later, while painting the outside of the building, he accidentally broke one of the upstairs windows, but refused to go in and mend it. He mended it from the outside instead, and left the broken glass all over the attic floor. That night, people heard strange noises in the attic. When they went upstairs the next morning, the floor was clean and all the broken glass was tidily in a corner.

Even today, hotel guests report hearing light footsteps in the attic, and moaning is often heard coming from behind a curtain in the dining room. Many people also report seeing an elderly woman looking out of an attic window. She's very popular with both local people and hotel guests.

2 Rewrite the sentences about Dover Castle using the phrases below. Use the text about Heceta Head Lighthouse to help you.

a People say that the castle is the home of many ghosts.
It is said that . . . the castle is the home of many ghosts.

b People say the headless ghost of a boy walks round the castle at night.
It is said . . .

c People think he is the ghost of Sean Flynn, a 15-year-old drummer boy.
It is thought . . .

d The ghosts of World War II soldiers haunt the tunnels under the castle.
The tunnels . . .

e Many visitors say that they have heard the noise of running boots in these tunnels.
Many visitors report hearing . . .

f Castle workers say that the king's bedroom is haunted by the lower half of a man.
It . . .

g People think that the ghost of a Roman soldier haunts the castle gardens.
It . . .

h Many people say they have seen a mysterious woman in red on one staircase.
Many people report . . .

i People often hear the noise of a door opening and closing in a place where there isn't a door any more.
The noise . . .

3 Rewrite this text in an impersonal style using passives and *report* + *–ing*.

Moravian Cemetery

Staten Island, New York

People think that this cemetery dates back to the time of the first Dutch settlers on Staten Island. The famous Vanderbilt Tomb stands in one corner of the cemetery and many people believe that it is haunted. Many people say that they have seen ghosts near the tomb. People have also heard crying and moaning noises coming from inside. People say that many photos taken in front of the tomb have an unknown person in the picture. One woman says that she took a photo of her family in front of the tomb, but when she got home there was no one in the picture.

4 Complete the table below about one of these haunted places.

- a haunted building near where you live
- a famous haunted building in your country
- a haunted building from a horror film
- your own invented haunted building

Name of building	
Location	
History of building	
Description of ghost	
Story of ghost's past	
Ghost's activities	
People's feelings	

5 Write a short text about your haunted building for a *Haunted Places* website.

GRAMMAR CHECK

Past Simple, Past Perfect, and Past Continuous

We use the Past Simple to talk about past actions that follow each other in a story.

He passed through me and disappeared out of the window.

We use the Past Perfect for actions that happened *before* an action in the past.

Before I met Johnson I had only read ghost stories.

We use the Past Continuous for a longer action that happens at the same time as a short action.

He was coming out of my room when I first saw him.

while often introduces the Past Continuous.

While I was standing there, Johnson passed through me.

when often introduces the Past Simple.

He was moaning when he disappeared out of the window.

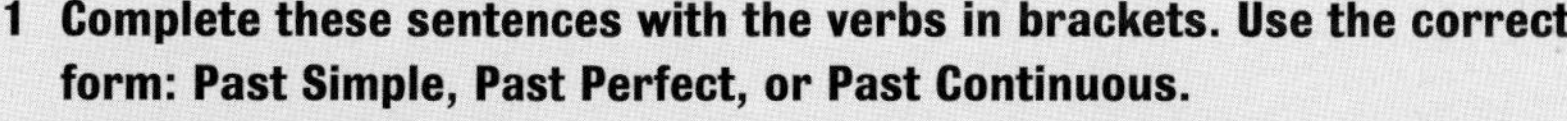

1 Complete these sentences with the verbs in brackets. Use the correct form: Past Simple, Past Perfect, or Past Continuous.

- **a** While the boy ..was going.. (go) to bed, he felt afraid.
- **b** The boy and his father .... (eat) when they spoke about the ghost.
- **c** Years before the story began, Johnson .... (love) a woman by the name of Emily.
- **d** Emily's family .... (leave) the house by the time Johnson came back.
- **e** When the family .... (meet) Johnson at first, they walked round him.
- **f** When the family .... (feel) comfortable with Johnson, they walked through him.
- **g** Johnson was very noisy one night while the family .... (play) a game of cards.
- **h** When the family .... (try) to find Emily's grave, they couldn't.
- **i** The family put a gravestone on the grave after the workmen .... (finish) digging it.
- **j** When Johnson .... (saw) Emily's name on the gravestone, he ran to it.
- **k** While Dad and old Squibbins .... (watch) Johnson by Emily's grave, they started to cry.

GRAMMAR

GRAMMAR CHECK

Past Simple: active and passive

We use the Past Simple active when we are interested in the person *doing* the action.

Dumoise worked as a doctor in the Punjab.

We use the Past Simple passive when we are interested in the *action*, not who did it.

Dumoise's wedding was held at the British church in Meridki.

Different friends were invited.

The word by can introduce the person who did the action.

Ram Dass was employed by Mrs Dumoise.

2 Complete these sentences with the verbs in brackets. Use the correct form: Past Simple Active or Passive.

a Dumoise married (marry) a round, sleepy-looking woman.
b Dumoise and his wife .... (shut) themselves away from the world.
c Meridki .... (hit) by a typhoid epidemic.
d The illness .... (catch) by many people.
e Mrs Dumoise .... (die) of it.
f Dumoise .... (take) away from his wife's grave.
g He .... (tell) to take a holiday.
h He .... (decide) to go on a walking tour.
i He .... (hope) to take lots of photographs and to forget his grief.
j Ram Dass .... (give) everything to manage on the tour.
k Mrs Dumoise's ghost .... (speak) to Ram Dass.
l A telegram .... (send) from the government offices in Simla.
m Dumoise .... (order) to go to Nuddea.
n Ram Dass .... (pay) by Dumoise.
o A reference .... (write) for him.
p Dumoise .... (kill) in a cholera epidemic.

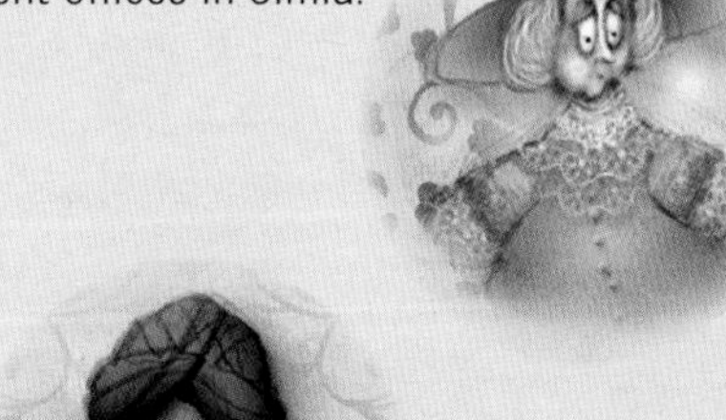

GRAMMAR CHECK

Used to/Use to

Used to/use to refers to past habits.

+ *As a child, the baron's daughter used to study with her aunts.*

– *She didn't use to meet any young men.*

? *Did she use to go horse riding?*

3 Complete the text from the diary of the baron's daughter. Use the verbs from the box in the *used to* form.

be	dream	not get	have	not leave	~~listen to~~	live
	obey	play	read	sing	wear	

When I was younger, I a) used to listen to everything that my aunts told me. I b)........................ the castle alone. I c)........................ dancing lessons and I d)........................ the guitar. I e)........................ beautiful songs, too. I f)........................ into trouble. I g)........................ lots of sensible books. I h)........................ very polite and I i)........................my father. I j)........................the sensible clothes that my aunts chose for me. I k)........................a very quiet life. I l)........................ of love in my bed at night.

4 Write sentences or questions about the Baron's daughter as a child. Use the words in brackets with *used to, didn't use to,* or *did...use to?*

a (live exciting life) She didn't used to live an exciting life .

b (wear sensible shoes) ....

c (read love stories).. .

d (sing love songs).. ?

e (use bad language).. .

f (play card games).. ?

g (dream of marrying a good-looking man).. .

GRAMMAR CHECK

Gerund with sense verbs

We use the –ing verb form (the gerund) with verbs of the senses like *hear, see, feel* and *smell*, and also verbs like *watch, listen to* and *notice*.

They heard somebody playing a horn at the castle gate.

5 Complete the sentences about the ghostly bridegroom with the Past Simple form of the verbs in the box.

feel	hear	listen to	not notice	~~not hear~~	see	watch

a The ghostly bridegroom didn't hear the baron welcoming him very clearly.

b He .... his young bride slowly arriving with her aunts.

c He .... the faces in the pictures on the wall looking down at him.

d He .... the servants putting food in front of him because he was busy with his bride.

e He .... people whispering around him.

f He .... the baron telling ghost stories with interest.

g He .... the cold wind blowing on his face.

6 Complete the sentences about the bride with the *–ing* form of the verbs in the box.

leave	look	shake	sigh	~~stand~~
talk	wave	whisper		

a The bride saw the bridegroom standing in front of her.

b She heard one of her aunts .... something in her ear.

c She listened to her bridegroom .... softly and sweetly.

d She watched him .... around the hall out of the corner of her eye.

e She felt herself .... nervously.

f She heard her bridegroom .... deeply.

g She watched him .... goodbye.

h She saw him .... the room.

GRAMMAR CHECK

Echo questions

We ask echo questions to show interest in what someone has said to us.

The subject and verb in the echo question match the subject and verb in the sentence.

A: The doll's house was an 18th century one.

B: Was it?

7 Complete the conversation with the echo questions in the box.

Did he?	~~Did he?~~	Did it?	Did she?	Did they?
Was he?	Was it?	Was she?	Were there?	Were they?

A: Mr Dillet bought an old doll's house.

B: a) Did he?

A: He did. There were twelve dolls in it, too.

B: b) ....

A: Yes. The Chittendens were happy to sell the thing to him.

B: c) ....

A: They were. Because it was haunted.

B: d) ....

A: Yes. Every night it came to life.

B: e) ....

A: It did, and Mr Dillet was able to see the story of an old murder in it.

B: f) ....

A: Yes. The woman in blue murdered the old man in his four-poster bed, you see.

B: g) ....

A: She did, and she was his daughter.

B: h) ....

A: Yes, and then the old man killed his grandchildren.

B: i) ....

A: He did. Then later Mr Chittenden and Mr Dillet talked about what they'd seen.

B: j) ....

GRAMMAR CHECK

Direct and reported speech

In direct speech we give the words that people say.	In reported speech we put the verb one step into the past and change the pronouns and the possessive adjectives.
'My name's Jack Collis,' he said.	*He said that his name was Jack Collis.*
'The statues have moved!' he said.	*He said that the statues had moved.*

We use statement word order and sentence construction to report questions.

'Where do you live?' I asked her. *I asked her where she lived.*

8 Rewrite direct speech as reported speech.

a 'What's the matter?' Jack asked Laura.

Jack asked Laura what the matter was.

b 'Someone has turned Mrs Dorman against us,' said Laura to Jack.

....

c 'We won't have time for writing and painting,' Laura told Jack.

....

d 'I'll speak to Mrs Dorman when she comes back,' said Jack.

....

e 'Aren't you happy here with us?' Jack asked Mrs Dorman.

....

f 'Why don't you want to stay with us?' Jack asked Mrs Dorman.

....

g 'You and your wife have always been good to me,' Mrs Dorman told Jack.

....

h 'My niece is ill,' said Mrs Dorman.

....

i 'I'm not like other people who laugh at strange old stories,' Jack said.

....

j 'Where do the statues go?' asked Jack.

....